SPICED UP!

SPICED UP!

· ·

MY MAD YEAR WITH
THE SPICE GIRLS

Muff Fitzgerald

Hodder & Stoughton

Copyright © Muff Fitzgerald 1998
Illustration 'Hello Brown Eye' copyright Harry Borden

First published in Great Britain in 1998
by Hodder and Stoughton
A division of Hodder Headline PLC

The right of Muff Fitzgerald to be identified as the Author of
the Work has been asserted by him in accordance with the Copyright,
Designs and Patents Act 1988.

10 9 8 7 6 5 4 3 2 1

British Library Cataloguing in Publication Data
A CIP catalogue record for this title is available
from the British Library.

ISBN 0 340 717629

Typeset by
Hewer Text Ltd, Edinburgh
Printed and bound in Great Britain by
Mackays of Chatham PLC, Chatham, Kent

HODDER AND STOUGHTON
A division of Hodder Headline PLC
338 Euston Road
London NW1 3BH

Dedicated to those who left the party early:

Tim Nicholson, Lee Newman, Roger 'Wildchild' McKenzie, James Dickens, Glenn Churchman and Kathy Acker.

ACKNOWLEDGEMENTS

· ·

A HEARTFELT THANK YOU TO: THE THREE JEWELS: BUDDHA, DHARMA, SANGHA; MALU HALASA – FOR HER UNFAILING SUPPORT OVER THE YEARS, WITH HER ENTHUSIASTIC ENCOURAGEMENT FOR ME TO BECOME A WRITER; JODY DUNLEAVY; MY TWO DADS: EDWARD 'NED' FRANCIS AND DADDY LOUIS; ME DEAR BRO GEOFF; MARILLA; DANIEL FITZGERALD; JULIAN ALEXANDER – THE BEST AGENT IN THE UNIVERSE!, KIRSTIN ROMANO; ATULA; FRANCIS SELF; DANAVIRA; RAY BURMISTON; DANIEL NEWMAN; TIM JEFFERY; MALCOLM 'GHOST SPELLER' DUFFY; BERNI KILMARTIN; GEORGIA GARRETT; SIMON PROSSER; NEIL TAYLOR; DEREK RIDGERS; PETE HUGGINS; STEWART READ; PETER BARNES; MAYLIN LEE; CHRIS HEATH; PETER LORRAINE; TONY FARSIDES; LOUISE GANNON; JULIAN BARTON; VERONICA HOWARD; YOSHKA RAMELOW; SYBIL RUSKILL; DI CARTER; ANNA; MAIRIE; JANET; BETTY AND THE GANG; DENNIS COCKELL; NORA BELTON; HJORDIS; DUFFOS; ANNOS AND NICOS; CHRISTINE AND UWE; THE MANUMISSION FAMILY; THE VERY REVEREND AL GREEN; LOVERS AND GROOVERS EVERYWHERE: BUT MOST OF ALL MY LOVELY MUM, CARMEL!

CONTENTS

• •

FOREWORD

· ·

If an alien had landed on Earth over the last couple of years and asked which humanoids were the most vital to meet and spend time with, it's a fair bet that the resounding answer would have been The Spice Girls.

They appeared from nowhere and in the space of a few short months they captured the imagination and hearts of people all over the planet, in the process becoming icons and players on the world's stage; boldly writing their names into the history books with indelible lipstick while noisily inviting all and sundry to join them in their rallying cry of Girl Power!

The Spice Girls have made their mark as the greatest cultural phenomenon since The Beatles, held up globally as examples of British excellence, achieving such mythic status that Mongol tribesmen in the Gobi Desert have been heard to utter the names Posh, Sporty, Ginger, Scary and Baby in the same breath as George Best and Paul McCartney.

Something like this occurs only once in a lifetime and, for some unknown reason, the powers in the universe decided that I would be lucky enough to work with The Girls for a year, sharing their experiences and taking part in the maddest adventure of my life.

This book is the story of that year, an exhausting time crammed full of unique never-to-be-repeated moments and more surprises than I ever thought possible. I'd like to take you behind the scenes and share my year with you. I hope you enjoy it.

As Victoria would say, hang on to your knickers!, it's gonna be a bumpy ride!

Chapter One

●●●●●●●●●●●●●●●●●●●●●●●●●●●●●●●●●●●●●●

WELCOME TO SPICE WORLD!

London, May, 1996

It's hard to believe today that I left The Spice Girls. It seems like just five minutes ago that I was exploring the delicate parameters of my duties on my very first assignment with The Girls: standing in a freezing field at six in the morning, bent over, with my trousers round my ankles, pointing my twin moons at the five most famous faces on the planet, while, amid their animated cat-calls and wolf-whistles, Geri shouted: 'Hello, brown eye!'

Who would have thought that after such a distinguished introduction and four thousand, seven hundred and fourteen hours of hair and make-up, not to mention three and a quarter million air-miles, two untoward incidents of fisticuffs with pa-parazzi, and one bout of nervous exhaustion later, I would be telling Posh, Sporty, Ginger, Scary and Baby that I would be leaving.

I had been working as a press officer at their record label, Virgin, for a year when I was given the honour of working the company's latest success. The Spice Girls had just gone to

1

Number One with 'Wannabe' when I was asked to handle their publicity. Little did I realise the day I started work, that I was about to be catapulted through the maddest year of my life: a year packed with glitz, glamour, paranoia, pursuit and ever increasing hysteria; a year that was to change their lives, and mine, for ever.

It was a year that saw The Spice Girls go from being complete unknowns to becoming the biggest pop phenomenon the world has known since The Beatles. A year that saw The Spice Girls achieve world domination and top the charts in thirty-three countries, selling seventeen million albums and fourteen million singles in the process.

So what, you may wonder, was I doing exposing my bottom to these gorgeous young women at that ungodly hour? My first assignation as The Spice Girls' publicist was to accompany a journalist and photographer from teen magazine *Big!* out to the middle of Hertfordshire, to cover a feature story with The Girls going up in a hot-air balloon with Denise Van Outen for ITV's *Massive* show. The best time for balloon flight is very early in the morning, before the air-currents have warmed up, something which makes landing more difficult.

Not unsurprisingly at six a.m., The Girls were tired and more than just half asleep. As the balloon wasn't going to be ready for half an hour, Harry Borden, the photographer, wanted to take a portrait of The Girls standing in a newly ploughed field, which was still being hugged by the early morning mist.

Victoria, who had been out with friends the night before, and like most of the other Girls that freezing day, was inappropriately dressed for the morning's endeavours in an outfit that consisted of wafer-thin slacks, black crop-top and matching jacket, exclaimed drily: 'I didn't think this pop star lark was going to be quite so glamorous,' as she distastefully wiped the mud off her Gucci loafers, and continued to drag herself dutifully behind the other four Girls into the middle of the field where the photographer had set up his tripod and camera. They were tired, they were freezing but, above all, The Spice Girls are dedicated and they remained uncomplainingly professional. However, they were still half-asleep.

'Muff, in the good interests of this project, why don't you surprise The Girls and do a moonie?' suggested Harry.

'What?' I exclaimed, not exactly awake myself.

'Go on, that'll get the sleep out of their eyes.'

Getting a premonition that from now on I was going to be required to perform actions like this that were above and beyond the call of one's everyday duties, I duly obliged and dropped my 501s to the aforementioned laughter and much girlie heckling.

'You're mad, you are,' shrieked Mel B, her huge and endearing Yorkshire laugh echoing from beneath the hood of her blue parka.

'Ooh, thank you!' I replied sarcastically.

'Thanks everyone, I got the shot,' shouted Harry, as we wrapped up and headed back towards the balloon.

Before we climbed into the basket, The Girls asked if anyone had any tissues with them and they departed into the bushes for a wee. This, it transpired, was a good idea, because once we were aboard and the balloon reached a height of two hundred feet, the air-currents changed and any thoughts we had of soon placing our feet on terra firma had to be dispensed with. For the next two hours we were at the mercy of the heavens, floating along without the means of making our descent.

'Can we get down now please?' Scary eventually asked in her I'm-being-polite-but-I'm-really-bored-now voice.

'I think I'm going to be sick,' added a pale-faced Victoria, wearily.

'Stick your head over the side, Vee,' advised Geri.

Baby was not happy either. 'It's bloody freezing up here.'

By the time we got down, The Girls were more than a little peed off.

In retrospect, this episode strikes me as an appropriate metaphor for the direction The Girls' lives was about to take. They willingly embarked on a journey that turned out to be monumental. It was to become the adventure of a lifetime, their lifetime and our lifetime, and one that would take them beyond the normal limits designated to pop stars and musicians. They would come to represent a generation and an era, remembered as much for their major cultural significance as for their music.

Like the incident with the balloon, once they had embarked on that journey, unseen forces conspired and took over: the momentum was swift and significant and even if The Girls had wanted to stop, or change direction, it would have been too late – the forces that forged their destiny were out of their hands.

I have this image of The Girls stuck in the balloon, but instead of a burner taking the balloon to new heights, the balloon is powered by their gushing enthusiasm and unbridled energy. They're all talking at once in their own inimitable, loquacious fashion, with their radiant charm and intense vitality propelling them ever higher and higher into the stratosphere. I see Scary Spice, head tilted back, yelling madly into the balloon: 'Aaaaaaaaaaaaaaaaaargh!'

In reality, that balloon journey was a turning point for The Girls. Their lives would never be the same from that moment on. For Victoria, Melanie C, Geri, Melanie B and Emma, the only way was up . . .

It was a fateful July day that I walked into my boss Robert Sandall's office at Virgin to be told that I would be working with The Spice Girls. My initial feeling was one of immense jubilation.

WOW! What a mind blast. I had been given the job every hot-blooded male in the country would give his eye teeth for. I was going to be handling The Spice Girls' press.

Since my first meeting with The Girls at a lunch with *Top Of The Pops* magazine a few months previously, I had been overwhelmed by their vivaciousness and enthusiasm for life and was struck by their fierce joy and dedication to the job they were doing.

This was followed by the feeling that a fully-laden double-decker bus was resting on the shoulders of my gingham Burberry button down (£16.99 at the Burberry factory shop!). The truth started to sink in: I had been given the company's flagship act to work. In exchange for that, before I left the building that day, I was required to deposit with the personnel department, one small detail: my life. The responsibility was enormous.

No more Buddhist retreats or meditation classes for me. No time to do anything but eat, breathe and sleep Spice Girls. As the *NME* later put it: 'Here is a man who cheerily admits that for the last three months he has thought nothing but Spice twenty-four hours a day.'

From the moment I took over the handling of their press, it became a twenty-four-hours-a-day, eight-days-a-week vocation. I had to forget about a personal life, The Girls' welfare was my primary concern.

The job was about protection as much as it was about promotion.

I was setting up interviews, trying to frighten off journalists who were door-stepping their families, arranging photo shoots, escorting journalists around the world to do stories on Our Girls. We worked most evenings and every weekend. The eighteen-hour days became the norm. Like Margaret Thatcher, we learned to cope with just four hours' sleep a night. I was away from home so much, even my mum forgot what I looked like.

In early September, as part of our promotion for The Girls' second single 'Say You'll Be There', which was due to be released on 14 October 1996, I arranged to take a journalist and the picture editor of *More!* magazine, the best-selling young women's magazine, to Los Angeles to do a shoot on trendy Venice Beach, the day before The Girls went into the Mojave Desert to shoot their video for the single.

I should have known what kind of a trip was in store when at the Virgin Atlantic check-in, my charges, Jordan Paramour and Holly Coles, when asked by the security man if they had anything dangerous in their bags replied with girlish giggles: 'No, just a bomb.'

Laugh? Ooh, the ripples were distinctly discernible as they went through our baggage with a fine toothcomb and gave us all a thorough body search. Mercifully, they spared us the rubber glove treatment and allowed us to depart with the tattered shreds of our dignity intact.

The next day, suffused with jet lag and Ernest and Julio Gallo's calling card throbbing through our temples, we got a cab from the Sunset Marquis Hotel on Sunset Boulevard down to Venice Beach. Venice Beach is a bit like Camden-On-Sea. A veritable wealth of tacky stalls selling T-shirts, hippy scarves and glasses, crystals and all the other accoutrements desired for either a New Age or stoned-age lifestyle. It is also known as Muscle Beach, because there are several outdoor gyms where pumped-up Michelin men huff and puff as their steroid-ridden bodies defy nature to lift weights that even a fork-lift truck might have a problem with.

The premise of our feature for *More!* magazine was thus: The Spice Girls were to be photographed visiting the stalls, having their tarot cards read, and posing with some of the colourful characters (i.e., freaks) that populate the area. They were also expected to do an a cappella busking session, just to see what the response was and how much money they could make.

After the session for *More!*, The Girls were to change into *Baywatch*-style swimming costumes and grab the lifeguard rafts for photos that would become the 'Spicewatch' poster and which we intended to use as exclusive shots for the *Sun*. And which indeed did eventually lead to The Girls making page three (again!).

We got there early to do a spot of shopping. I bought a Beavis and Butthead 'Tommy Pullmyfinger T-shirt'. Where were The Girls though? We thought they were late, but after searching all over the place we spotted their land-cruiser parked behind the racquet ball courts.

The five Girls came pouring out of the bus, all smiles, all talking at once and absolutely raring to go. Earlier that morning some monks from a Shaolin Temple had been teaching them some kung-fu moves for their video and The Girls were still really fired up, demonstrating the lethal moves they'd been practising.

We ran through what we wanted them to do for the feature, first getting The Girls to pose in front of a huge mural that dominates the sidewalk.

'They're really nice. They're not at all what I expected,' said Holly. 'They're really up for it aren't they?'

When The Girls go to work, *they go to work!*

I took a few minutes to describe The Girls to Holly. If I'd known them then as well as I know them now, here's what I would have said to her.

Firstly there's Geri.

Geri is a couple of years older than the other Girls and because of that she is inclined to seize the initiative and almost always assumes responsibility for the group. She tends to be the self-appointed spokesperson, though sometimes this annoys the other Girls in the group because they all like to have their opinions heard and noted. It is after all a democracy.

enthusiasm personified. She has a keen, enquiring
a natural hunger for knowledge, whether it is internal,
ng for self-knowledge, or always eager to learn about the
genous people and cultures of the countries she travels to in
the course of her job. Which is a lot. Believe me. The VIP unit at
Heathrow said they've never known any band travel as exten-
sively or as often as The Spice Girls.

She is very close to her mother Anna-Maria and her biggest
regret is that her dad, Laurence, who died at the age of seventy-
one, didn't witness her success as a Spice Girl. The Jaguar tattoo
she has at the base of her back is in memory of her father, who was
a car salesman for Jaguar. Geri's lived life more than a little and
therefore her self-assurance may occasionally come across as
bossiness.

She loves life and she throws herself into her work. She is
dedicated to it and takes a genuine interest in it. Before Geri does
an interview with a journalist she makes a point of reading any
books or articles they have written. The day of the Brit Awards,
after the dress rehearsal, while some of the other Girls went home
or went shopping, Geri stayed behind in the dressing room and
put in an extra hour's dance tuition with Priscilla, her choreographer. After the performance she was really pleased and 'felt
that that extra time really paid off'.

Geri is extremely polite to everyone she comes into contact
with and has a filthy and sometimes absurd sense of humour,
which is terribly endearing. She is top.

Victoria.

Victoria is also extremely hard working. She has a very witty
and dry sense of humour and there is a beautiful sense of
equilibrium about her. She is very even tempered and maintains
her good humour and enthusiasm throughout even the most
adverse, exhausting or just plain boring situations. She trained as
a dancer and loves music: good garage and quality soul music.

She used to love going clubbing, but sadly with celebrity, her clubbing has suffered and it's difficult to go out without being bothered all night, not to mention the interminable chase home by the paparazzi. She's very close to all of her family and when she's not out of the country, she lives at home with her mum and dad, Jacqui and Tony, and brother, Christian and sister, Louise.

Victoria is definitely not posh, however she has a markedly refined aesthetic sensibility. Her taste in clothes and design is very sophisticated. She adores the finer things in life. She says in a lot of aspects her life is very much the same as it was before she joined The Spice Girls, only now she has twenty-five pairs of Gucci shoes instead of one. Victoria prefers films to books, has a very good eye and has said that when The Spice Girls (God forbid!) finally split up, she would like to open her own art gallery and also a restaurant. She is a little darling and was always a pleasure to be around.

Melanie B.

Melanie is imbued with a very big and equally warm heart. She can be overpoweringly enthusiastic about things and burns with an almost incandescent energy. By contrast she also likes periods of quiet and introspection. Those times when she can take her make-up off, put her feet up and just be herself are not only important to her, but vital and extremely nourishing. She has a meditation chair at home. She loves her family deeply and is also very generous. As soon as she got her first royalty cheque the first thing she did was buy her mum, Andrea, a car. A little later on when she first had the time, she threw a big party at a club in Leeds and invited all her close friends and family and all the people who'd given her support throughout her life.

More than anything she hates people to think she's stupid, which most definitely she is not. Melanie is a very intelligent woman and her shouty behaviour is sometimes misinterpreted by people as being somewhat foolhardy; far from it, she should never be underestimated. She is incredibly hard working, sometimes a bit impatient but at the same time always earnest. She has single-handedly revived the fortunes of leopard-print manufacturers around the world. She loves music, tuff and ruff drum 'n' bass and Prince and Jamiroquai, or Jay Kay as she likes to call him. I like her very much and at the risk of sounding a complete old fogey, she really reminds me of myself, particularly when I was her age.

Melanie C.

Melanie C, despite her initial boyish image, in many ways is probably the softest and warmest of all five Girls. She is very down to earth, extremely grounded, has a very practical outlook on life and is always very friendly, though she can be quite shy and reserved with people she doesn't know.

Melanie is very self-disciplined and works extremely hard on maintaining a level of fitness that would put most athletes to shame. Her body is a temple. She hates formality of any kind and doesn't have time for hot-air merchants, of which there are a lot in the music industry. She's football mad and has a keen appreciation of all sport.

Since joining The Spice Girls she has really come into her own and blossomed. It's been a joy to watch her grow and develop. She's very close to her family, her mum, Joan, who is also a singer; her dad, Alan and her younger brother Paul. She accepts the level of media interest in her as part of her job, but quite naturally resents the intrusion on the lives of the people she loves.

Melanie adores music, is an absolutely wicked dancer and the other Girls say she is the most musical of all of them and has the strongest voice. She has been called Indie Spice, because of her love of bands like the Manic Street Preachers, Radiohead and Blur. She was made up to have hung out with the Manic Street Preachers at the 1997 Brit Awards, but actually felt a bit guilty that The Spice Girls stole all the attention despite the Manics also winning two awards. She can be quite self-deprecatory at times.

She is very close to Emma and acts like her big sister. I think she would make a brilliant big sister for anyone to have.

Emma.

Emma's nickname is Baby Spice and she really is the baby of the group. She is the youngest and probably the quietest of The Girls. She is very in touch with her emotions and is the most likely to have a little cry when things get a bit too stressful or she gets tired. She is very close to her mum, Pauline, who teaches karate. Emma seems always to have her mobile phone glued to her ear to share with Pauline, who is her best friend, whatever exciting things are happening to her. She lives at home with Pauline and her brother Paul.

Back on Venice Beach I felt like I'd just discovered five little sisters, all different, who provoke that emotional bond that is particular to families. That's how I felt about The Girls, but I had the impression that when it came to their feelings towards me, it was somehow like they were a gang of schoolgirls, so close they didn't let anyone else into their gang, but they tolerated one or two older lads being around them, just in case there was any trouble. It's like: 'You're all right, otherwise we wouldn't let you hang around us. But don't think we're letting you join our gang, 'cause we're not!'

On the way to the tarot reader, Mel C and Victoria complimented me on my new tattoo. I had just had the outline done on my arm of Green Tara, a Buddhist spiritual archetype: the Bodhisattva of compassion. It took two hours and I had another sixteen hours to go before it would be finished and finally coloured in.

'That's the nicest tattoo I think I've ever seen,' said Victoria.

'Yeah, it's amazing,' added Melanie C.

I thanked The Girls and told Melanie C. I really liked her Celtic band tattoo and asked her how long it took and whether it hurt?

'It took about an hour and it really hurt on the inside of my arm, on the muscle,' she informed me with one of her disarming smiles.

Melanie B bounced over. 'Cor, I like that, Muff,' she said. 'Who is it?' Having missed the conversation with Victoria and Melanie C, I repeated who Green Tara is.

'Why did you want to have her on your arm then?' she asked. I replied that I feel a deep resonance with Green Tara and that having her tattooed on my arm involved an element of devotion.

'There's an element of devotion involved with my tattoo as well,' she said with a saucy grin, pointing down to some Japanese symbols below her belly button.

The tarot card reader had gone for a hot dog, so we traipsed over to Captain Jim, a salty ex-sea dog and palmist who, for the princely sum of eighty dollars, agreed to read the pretty hands of these five 'crazy English ladies' to see what their future would hold.

'Let me see,' he intoned mystically. 'You are all in a band and in six months from now, not only will you have the Number One single on the American Billboard chart, but your album *Spice* will be Number One here as well!'

Err, actually he didn't say that at all, but Jim was quite perceptive about one thing. He told them they would all have trouble with their relationships.

In a matter of months, every single boyfriend whom The Girls had ever had, – thirteen, in total – would have sold their stories to the newspapers.

Despite this prophetic piece of information, the up mood prevailed and we descended on the open-air gym where Dave, a veritable Colossus of a man, whose muscles had muscles had muscles and who was finishing off a workout, had promised us the use of his body for our photo shoot.

This guy looked like he ate steroids for breakfast, lunch, tea, dinner and a bedtime snack. Think Superman meets King Kong meets the Incredible Hulk. He was enormous and covered completely in Baby Oil. He lifted Victoria and Emma up, one in each hand, while Melanies B and C draped themselves around him and Geri, the ever saucy little minx, took him from behind and popped her head between his legs.

'My bum is all greasy now,' moaned Victoria.

'Yeah, so's mine! Can we go back to the land-cruiser to get a towel to wipe this oil off please?' Emma asked.

'I'm covered in it,' said Melanie C, 'I'm all for fitness and keeping your body in shape, but that . . . that was horrible.'

After a swift wipe-down, I asked The Girls if they'd now like to do the busking.

Geri was not up for it at all. 'I just think it would be really tacky, you know,' she said, taking the lead in her husky voice.

She rallied the other Girls around her for a quick conflab. The Girls' decision was democratic and it was final. No. Too tacky.

While we thought about an alternative, we were approached by a group of English tourists on holiday who couldn't believe their luck. The Spice Girls! In the flesh! While The Girls were still unknown in America, they had just been Number One in Britain for seven weeks. The Girls signed autographs while I asked Venice Beach's 'famous' One Man Band if he would mind if I gave him some money and The Girls posed with his instruments for a couple of minutes and pretended to busk. He was cool with that, though a little bemused by The Girls, as were the interested crowd who quickly gathered around them. Personally I think it would have been less tacky for The Girls to perform their 'One Of These Girls', a cappella which had been their party piece for the past year, but once they make their mind up about something, despite it being a real Lay-Dee's prerogative, they rarely change it.

We are joined at this point by Simon Fuller, The Spice Girls' manager. Simon is the astute, fresh-faced, thirty-six-year-old shrewd Svengali who was well on the way to becoming one of those legendary figures like Colonel Tom Parker or Brian Epstein. He was here to oversee the 'Spicewatch' shoot. The Girls finished 'busking', I paid the (one) Man (band) fifty dollars and we went back to the land-cruiser so The Girls could change into their swimming costumes.

One by one The Girls jumped out of the cruiser. To say the bright red one-piece costumes were revealing is something of an understatement. They were so revealing, that that morning, before the kung-fu lessons, each Girl had to have a special bikini-line wax at their posh LA abode, the Four Seasons Hotel.

The reason The Girls were at the Four Seasons Hotel and we were at the Sunset Marquis was because it was management policy that journalists never stayed in the same hotel as the band on a trip. This was to guarantee The Girls more than a modicum of privacy and also, The Girls being *The Girls!*, whenever anyone from the media or the business is around, they just do not stop working. It's in their nature as compulsive workaholics.

Each Girl's costume was adorned by a whistle and Geri also donned a red baseball cap. Geri, Melanie B and Melanie C, kept their trainers on (just like they would in *Baywatch!*), while Emma wore her platform white sandals. Victoria felt quite embarrassed by the revealing nature of the skimpy swimsuit, holding her red plastic lifeguard raft alternately behind her bum or in front of her nether regions as we walked towards an abandoned lifeguard tower a few hundred yards from the land-cruiser.

The Girls ran up the stairs to the tower and posed for the first set of photos. Victoria also had a pair of binoculars around her neck which she used to scour the shoreline for any sign of trouble. And trouble was on its way, sure enough.

As The Girls lined up on the beach to do the shot that would become the image that adorned bedroom walls all over the world, a four-wheel drive vehicle approached from another lifeguard post half a mile down the beach. A uniformed lifeguard official jumped out of the jeep and asked us 'What the hell do you think you're doing?', followed by an immediate request to see our permit.

Before any of us could reply, Geri, as ever, steamed in: 'Oh, officer, we're just a gang of mates on holiday having a laugh and taking a few snapshots for our friends and families back home,' before adding with her cutest, most flirtatious eyelids-fluttering and bottom-wobbling look, 'We're not here professionally or anything.'

At this, the officer retorted rather curtly: 'Well, it looks very professional to me.'

At any other time I would have taken this as a compliment, but right then, maybe not so. It was time to bite the bullet. I introduced myself and told him I worked for Virgin Records, and that we were really sorry, we didn't mean to cause any trouble or bring lifeguards or the essential and absolutely life-saving work they did into disrepute in any way, shape or form.

'That's as may be,' he replied in his best John Wayne voice, 'but do you have a permit registered with the Sheriff's Office to shoot here on the beach?'

'Well, not personally, but I'm sure my company Virgin do, as they shoot all over LA all the time.' Thinking that since this was America, the land of the free and the land where dead presidents ruled supreme, I pulled out my tour float and asked whether I could make a donation to the Lifeguards' Fund?

This was definitely a bad move. His features grew ever more tactiturn and, angrily declining my offer, he said he would have to check whether we had a permit and under no circumstances were we to do anything till he came back.

As soon as his wheels spun off down the beach, Geri shouted: 'Quick, let's do these bloody shots before he comes back!'

Gathering the other Girls into position, they stood in a line and positioned their legs like a group of latter-day Tiller Girls, Simon and the photographer both clicking away.

By the time the officer returned we had finished.

'It's OK,' he said. 'Virgin Records are registered with the Sheriff's Office. Have a good time.'

The Girls asked him to pose with them for a photo but he declined. So they gave a resounding chorus of THANK YOUs!!! and off he drove into the distance.

The Girls were always very appreciative and they always made people around them feel affirmed; they made a point of saying an emphatic 'Thank You' to whoever had done whatever for them. They are very polite young women.

After The Girls changed out of their costumes, we did the one thing that they love even more than working: SHOPPING!

We trawled down the promenade, Emma buying some baby-blue sunglasses. There was a lack of designer boutiques and sports shops down there, so Victoria and Melanie C were out of luck. Melanie B bought some incense and Geri got a couple of tops.

Clutching their purchases and with a goodbye and a big THANK YOU! to Jordan and Holly, The Girls were back on the land-cruiser and on the way back to the exclusive confines of the Four Seasons Hotel.

Holly, Jordan and I slumped in a promenade café imbibing more Ernest and Julio Gallo. We were absolutely exhausted. The Girls were FAB, but it was bloody tiring being with them.

When we got back to the UK, our promotion for 'Say You'll Be There' and *Spice*, The Girls' debut album, which was due for release in early November, gathered pace.

It had always been Virgin's intention to place The Girls before the broadest demographic in press-media terms, a plan that was made ever more important after the initial snubbing that The Spice Girls endured by the teen press. Initially the teen press had a very snobby attitude, saying to a man (or woman) that girl bands never worked and that this outfit would prove no different. When 'Wannabe' knocked Gary Barlow off the top spot and kept Robbie Williams and George Michael at Number Two, how symbolic was that? The public chose what they really wanted and what they wanted was Girl Power!

We set out on a mission to entice the style press, the music press and those rather large organs of mass-media: the tabloid press.

In the record industry, the records are sold into the shops three or four weeks before release. When a band is hot, or when there's a significant groundswell or word-of-mouth buzz going down, it's usually reflected in the 'pre-sale' figure. That is the number of records the shops order to have in their stores ready for the day of release. In promotion terms, when this is a good figure, it can be wielded like a magical amulet. It can make things happen.

A lot of people within the industry were completely surprised by the enormous success of 'Wannabe'. The cynics (and there are quite a few of those around) had decided that The Spice Girls were a flash in the pan, an aberration, and that 'Wannabe' was a one-hit wonder. Of course, everyone connected with The Girls and everyone at Virgin knew this to be the furthest from the truth. After all, we had all heard the album and, above all, we were intimate with our biggest secret weapon: The Girls themselves.

Originally, Virgin weren't sure that 'Wannabe' should be the first single. They thought about putting out another track instead but The Girls vetoed that, put their platformed feet down and insisted on 'Wannabe' coming out as the first single.

Eight million sales later and I think they may have been right.

Similarly, with the video for 'Wannabe'. The senior management at Virgin weren't completely happy with the video and wanted to do a re-shoot. To be fair to them, they just wanted to be sure that when everything was ready to go, it was all perfect. Once again, The Girls stomped their feet and insisted that it was fine and to go with it. It became the most ever requested video on The Box cable channel in the UK and played a major part in the initial success of 'Wannabe'.

Despite being Number One for seven weeks, a lot of people in the media still weren't convinced, so, the day The Girls came in with the largest ever pre-sale of 334,000 records for 'Say You'll Be There', beating Virgin's previous record which was for George Michael's 'Jesus To A Child', I was on the phone letting this figure work its magic.

With a magic number like that, it was virtually definite that The Spice Girls were going to go straight in at Number One. Boyzone were set to release their single 'Words' the same day as 'Say You'll Be There', but their pre-sale was nowhere near as high as The Girls'. I felt twelve years old again, and remembered when Slade and The Sweet would put records out at the same time.

The Face eventually said they would like to do a feature. We were jubilant. A feature in the *The Face*, is the ultimate endorsement and is worth its weight in gold as a promotional and marketing tool.

The buzz started circulating through the media's luncheon rooms and drinking dens. The finished video, which was nothing short of a masterpiece, arrived from the editing suite and was released to television, later going on to win a Brit Award for Best Video.

On 8th October, the *Guardian* printed a story confirming that William Hill had announced The Spice Girls as the favourite for the Christmas Number One spot, going from twenty-five to one outsiders to six to one favourite. Everyone at work who'd had the good sense to get their money down at the earlier price walked round for days like Cheshire cats.

Although we were deep in the throes of advance promotion for both 'Say You'll Be There' and *Spice*, at this point we had also begun to make plans for our full-on Christmas assault, with Number One single and album being our ultimate goal. If we could achieve that it would be like winning the League and the FA cup. The double-bubble indeed!

We had an All-Departments Spice Girls' Planning Meeting every two weeks; present would be all the heads of departments and also Virgin's top brass: Paul Conroy (then managing director of Virgin, now president), Ray Cooper, (then joint assistant MD, later to become joint MD, and recently departed to become joint MD of Virgin America), Ashley Newton, the A&R man's A&R man (and like Cooper also joint assistant MD and also later joint MD of Virgin both in the UK and America) – the guy who signed The Girls to the label.

Also present were Simon Fuller, one of his staff and Nikki Chapman from Brilliant PR, The Girls' TV plugger, Nick Godwyn, also from Brilliant PR who was their radio plugger, plus regional promotions staff and staff from marketing and merchandise.

At these meetings every aspect of promotion and marketing was planned and discussed right down to the finest detail. From the artwork and type of mixes to be included on the record, to press, television and radio campaigns and what sort of fillings to have in the sandwiches at the launch party.

The odds on '2 Become I' were mentioned to a rather gleeful reception, which gave the meeting a rather premature, though not unlikely, celebratory atmosphere. Ray Cooper jocularly said that we might have to watch out for Catherine Cookson's version of 'My Way'.

Later that same week, Geri made the tabloid press for the first time when at the National Television Awards, where The Girls picked up the award on behalf of *Top Of The Pops* for best music show, she did a karate kick to the assembled photographers, which resulted in a rather candid photo of her nether regions. The papers claimed she wasn't wearing any knickers, Geri said she had a tiny G-string on.

Incidents like this added to The Girls' notoriety and, in terms of credibility, it just made them appear sassier than ever. The Spice Girls are naturals at using their sex appeal as a marketing tool, in much the same way that the Sex Pistols used obnoxious behaviour.

However, later on this caused a few ripples within the internal dynamics of the group, when the full extent of Geri's glamour modelling career became clear.

The following week, Ross Jones, reviewing 'Say You'll Be There' in the *Guardian* wrote: 'Here's what we know about Spice Girls so far: they like a drink, they've got breasts and are not afraid to use them or show them.' He finished off by giving the record the thumbs up for its 'G-funk thud and girlish crooning.' While the *NME*'s Mark Sutherland, in an outspoken editorial, declared that: 'Pop is the new indie! Bands like The Spice Girls have become successful entirely on their own terms, even the teenmags have been too busy embarrassing themselves chasing after the long departed Brit-pop bandwagon to offer much encouragement. There can be little doubt who provides the best role models.'

Linda Duff, the *Daily Star*'s pop editor – who presided over the Rave column and who 'discovered The Spice Girls seven months before anyone else' – that week wrote a double-page spread on The Girls.

Rave's guide to being a Spicette included DO´s: Make as much of a din as you can everywhere you go, making sure you'll get noticed. WEAR sporty outfits if you feel more comfortable in them. TAKE a leak in a plant pot if you get caught short! DO a streak at least once every six months. SHOUT back at lads, making them wilt with witty put downs.

DON´TS: *Never* be afraid to flash your undies in a micro-skirt. BE sure not to blush in front of men on building sites. DON´T turn down the offer of cocktails from admirers in a bar when you're out with The Girls. YOU can't let a good-looking fella pass without pinching his bum!

The day we released 'Say You'll Be There' we also announced the fact that The Girls had been invited to turn on the Oxford Street Christmas lights. By Thursday, we had our mid-week chart position. There was only one number these Girls understood. Numero Uno!

The Spice Girls had made chart history with their massive sales and new entry position. They had become the first all-Girl group in history to go to Number One with their debut single. But this was still only the beginning – the fates had much more in store for them. But sadly, as they were about to find out, nothing in this world comes without a price, and Our Girls were about to pay heavily for being public figures with the complete erosion of their private lives by the tabloid press.

Chapter Two

● ●

A NICE DAY OUT DOWN AT THE *SUN* . . .

October 1996

As soon as 'Say You'll Be There' sashayed into the charts at Number One, I was thrown helpless and head on into the quagmire of servicing the daily needs of the tabloid press. The tabloids had woken up to the fact that Girl Power! had arrived, that it was what the public wanted and that putting The Spice Girls on their front pages would give an uplift in sales by at least ten per cent. My learning curve abruptly changed course and thrust itself towards the heavens.

Up until that point the national press had been ambivalent, patronisingly holding the view that The Spice Girls were really nothing more than a group of insubstantial, manufactured bimbos, one-hit-wonders who were to be occasionally patted on the head and humoured until the next big boy band sensation came along.

Fleet Street's finest had failed to grasp The Girls' mettle and aside from one or two throwaway picture captions and a double-page spread very early on in the *Daily Star*'s pop pages, most had failed to realise The Spice Girls' potential: apart from their glorious music, The Girls epitomised glamour galore, they were complete motormouths with an exuberant propensity towards a classic soundbite and they had become role models for at least half of the British female population. That, coupled with the fact that their story was fast becoming Britain's favourite soap opera, meant they now had a significance that was growing all the time.

If they'd been slow on the uptake till now, the tabloids certainly made up for lost time. Suddenly, every national newspaper was on the phone demanding an interview with The Spice Girls, insisting that we gave them information on their backgrounds, door-stepping their families and threatening all sorts of unpleasant stories if we refused to comply. And that was just the quality press. Hello, middle-market tabloids.

Dealing with the tabloid press was like juggling with a double-edged sword. We wanted the publicity, it was vital. If a story in a market-leading tabloid such as the *Sun* can reach thirty million people, well, there were thirty million reasons why we wanted The Girls to feature there. We wanted to achieve maximum exposure. But, of course, there was a price to pay. They might run a nice puff piece or feature our exclusive photos, but once the beast had awoken, it had to be fed constantly and while we were handing out tid-bits at the front door, the rest of the pack were clawing their way in through the back door.

Before I took up my post and learned how to walk with it, The Girls had featured twice in the *Sun*. The first time they had visited the *Sun*'s showbiz editor, Andy Coulson, at his home in Wandsworth, where he was in bed recovering from flu. The story had been along the lines of The Spice Girls making him feel much better. Victoria had pointed up at some decorative plasterwork on Coulson's ceiling and said to him: 'Ooh, I like your ceiling, Andy.' Whereupon he replied: 'Thank you! I've got my quote now . . .'

The second time was a picture-caption of The Girls with Chris Evans, taken backstage at GAY, a gay club in London, where they had just performed a PA. Evans had gone backstage to meet them and was chastised by them for repeatedly dissing them on his Radio 1 Breakfast show. (After this he started to play their records daily.)

Now that the *Sun*, like the rest of Fleet Street, had finally realised The Spice Girls' immense popularity, they wanted them to visit their Wapping HQ and edit the Bizarre column. We were in the thick of promoting 'Say You'll Be There' and the forthcoming album *Spice*, but we managed to squeeze an hour into an already jam-packed day.

It was October and just an average day for Posh, Ginger, Scary, Sporty and Baby Spice.

Up at six a.m., they were driven straight to *This Morning* with Richard and Judy at seven a.m., for hair, make-up and camera rehearsals. After performing 'Say You'll Be There' and being interviewed by their admiring hosts, they were to be taken to Wapping for photos and an interview at midday. At 1 o'clock, they were to be driven to Pinewood Studios at Elstree for that week's *Top Of The Pops*, to perform a version of 'Say You'll Be There'.

Following camera and sound clearance, which was expected at around eight o'clock, The Girls were to be whisked down the road to the Trust House Moat Hotel in Elstree, where, in the impromptu setting of the back bar, which had been converted into a photo studio for the evening, a cover shoot was to take place for the following week's issue of *Time Out*. The Girls were to finish shooting at about midnight, to be swept home in their fleet of sleek Jaguars to begin a similar schedule the following day. And the day after that. And the day after that. And the day after that.

Arriving at the Richard and Judy Show that morning, I was

greeted by a spine-tingling serenade of warm welcomes and charm-laden compliments that fluttered over me like confetti and, like a puppy whose eyes have just opened for the first time and to discover the magic and warmth of bright sunshine, I developed a huge grin and basked in the glow of The Girls' overwhelmingly seductive attention. They have this effect on everyone they meet.

'Ooh, you look really smart today.'

'I love that suit, is it Paul Smith?' enquired Victoria.

'Muff, thank you so much for that bottle of Rescue Remedy, it's brilliant stuff! It really works!' Geri exclaimed huskily as she bounced over on her Buffalo crepe platform shoes, puckering up and kissing me full on the lips, as was her disconcerting habit when she greeted those who worked with her regularly.

After such a greeting, all I really wanted was a little lie-down, but instead I gathered The Girls together in the Green Room and briefed them, all hugga-mugga, on our imminent visit to Fortress Wapping. I got a little paranoid when I realised that two gentlemen in the corridor outside were clocking every word of our conversation. But I relaxed when I found out they were fellow guests on the show and were in fact two hairdressers from Tunbridge Wells who'd created a revolutionary new haircare product which Richard and Judy's producers wanted them to try out on one of The Girls.

'God, I'm knackered,' exclaimed Baby a little while later in the car, as we sped away past the waiting fans gathered outside the London Television Centre, while she leaned down to rub a fleck of dirt off her blue knee-high suede boots, which contrasted with the lemon mini-dress she'd chosen to wear that morning.

'What else are we doing today?' she enquired sweetly as she snuggled up and rested her head on Mel's shoulder.

'After we go to the *Sun*, we've got *Top of The Pops* and then after that, tonight we're doing a shoot for *Time Out* for next week's cover.'

Mel's rich scouse accent bounced around the plush white leather seats. 'Eh, do you like this new Kappa tracksuit, they just sent me a whole box load. It's dead smart, eh?'

As usual when we tried to cram so much into a day, by the time we left Richard and Judy and had started motoring eastwards, we were running a little late. My mobile phone started to ring.

'Hello.'

'Muff? Andy! Where are you?'

'We're running a bit late, mate, we've just passed Stepney Green, we should be there in about ten minutes. Is everything OK?'

'Yeah, we're all ready for you, I'm gonna get Dominic [Dominic Mohan, one of Coulson's Bizarre team] to meet you at the gate and bring you all up.'

'OK. Cheers, mate. See you shortly.'

Coulson, aged twenty-nine, who edited the *Sun*'s infamous Bizarre showbusiness column, had worked his way up from the *Basildon Echo* and worked on the Bizarre column under Piers Morgan, when Kelvin MacKenzie ruled supreme in the editor's chair throughout the eighties.

Coulson commanded the ear of the now departed editor, Stuart Higgins and, apart from a short spell when he defected to the *Daily Mail*, which he disliked 'because of the old-school-tie network that operates there', he had made his name and somewhat fearsome reputation at the *Sun*.

With the demeanour of a slippery-scaled piranha, fond of wearing sharp suits and equally sharp-tongued or charming when he wanted to be, Coulson's entire raison d'être is to be first with 'The Story', whatever story is about to break and whomever he feels like elevating into news that week.

His middle name is 'Exclusive!'; his catch-phrase is 'You haven't done a deal with the *Mirror*, have you?'. He has the tenacity and persistence of a Rottweiler on dexedrine and he is extremely good at his job. Annoyingly so.

Having spoken only on the telephone so far, today was to be my first face-to-face meeting with him. He was about to become as familiar a feature in my life as my speaking 'No Smoking!' fridge magnet.

The Fab Five editing the Bizarre column entailed taking over Stuart Higgins's office and posing for photos in front of five 'Editor' signs the *Sun* had made specially for the occasion, plus a selection of other shots taken in and around the building, followed by a brief interview.

After crawling through lunchtime traffic, on arrival the atmosphere was somewhat akin to a royal visit. It appeared the entire staff of News International was hanging out of the windows, banners draped and cameras clicking, and a huge crowd had gathered around the entrance to the building. A young man in a grey suit and tie pushed through the crowd and greeted us as we spilled out of the convoy of Jags.

'Dominic?' I enquired politely, extending my hand.

'No: Andy!' he snapped back, touchily, obviously annoyed that I hadn't recognised him.

'Oh, mate, you look much younger than your picture in the column, it doesn't do you justice,' I retorted good-humouredly.

Oh dear. That was a good start. His face wrinkled in disgust and he hustled our mad circus of The Girls, PAs, hair-stylists, make-up artists and me through the crowd into a tiny lift and up into the offices of the *Sun*.

We were here at last. Inside the belly of the beast.

While The Girls were having their hair and make-up touched up, Coulson pulled me aside. 'You know the girls on the front page today, whom we just got released from Holloway? Well, they're here as well today and we thought it'd be a really good idea to take a picture of them with The Spice Girls. You can see the headline: ALL GIRLS TOGETHER! That sort of thing.'

The girls had been jailed for Contempt of Court for refusing to testify against their boyfriend, who had allegedly beaten them up. The *Sun* campaigned vigorously for their release, which had occurred the day before.

Feeling my heartbeat increase at this request, which was not exactly a dream photo-call, and fearing the imminent possibility of a stitch-up looming large, I took a deep breath: 'No, sorry, Andy. We're just here to edit the Bizarre column, mate.'

'Oh, come on! Just a little picture. Where's the harm in that?'

'Andy, we've come to edit your column, nothing else.'

'Where's the harm in it? Just a quick snap and that's it.'

'Look, I'll phone the management company and ask them, OK?'

I moved down the corridor for a bit of privacy. I was phoning just as a matter of form, to sweeten him up a bit, but I didn't expect the management to agree to it. They were appalled by the idea. It was a No.

'They said no, Andy.'

'Well, all right then, I'll just bring 'em down to say 'ello.' This idea also held less than zero appeal. If they were even in the same room together, I knew we'd be coerced into having the photo taken.

'No, Andy. We don't want to meet them. We don't even want them in the same room as us, OK?'

He was leaning into me now, face to face, in a defiant, hectoring manner. Here was a man who was used to getting his own way.

'What is the problem with that? They only want to say "ello?"

We were not getting anywhere here. I decided the best policy

was to ignore his verbal assault and I wandered off to see if The
Girls were almost ready.

They were ready. Camilla Howarth, one of The Girls'
personal assistants, came across and whispered, 'What's going
on?'

'I'll tell you later,' I whispered, more than a little on edge.

The Girls performed with their usual charm, wit and vigour,
equally aware that we were in the lion's den, but also that
although we were all on our guard, knew the power they
themselves held, and they could still have fun with the situation
and take the mickey just ever-so-slightly.

After we'd taken the pictures around the editor's desk,
Coulson asked Roger Crump, their photographer, to take a
shot of him kneeling in front of The Girls, hands held together
in a pleading gesture, with an expression of contrition and
repentance on his face.

Mel B was bang into it. 'Go on then, get down on yer knees!'
All The Girls stood around the now kneeling Coulson, wagging
their fingers mock-sternly, while he quipped: 'You know, there
are certain, ahem, gentlemen's magazines that would pay a lot of
money for photos like this.'

'Just shut up and look at the camera,' Scary bellowed in her
distinctive Yorkshire brogue, loving every minute of it.

While trying not to smile and while appreciating her typically
brave attitude, my mind was racing. While this would almost
definitely make a funny photo, why had Coulson requested it?
Was he going to run it as part of tomorrow's piece? What else had
he got up his sleeve? Why would he need to be seen apologising to
The Girls? Did he have some unsavoury story tucked away,
which after being published, he would follow up with a
BIZARRE TICKED OFF BY SPICE GIRLS! story, which
would make it seem as though he'd been forgiven and, hey,
they were all mates together again?

I had to calm down. It was just a harmless photo. I had to stop feeling so paranoid.

We finished shooting in the editor's office and then Coulson suggested doing some shots out by the Bizarre desk, which is situated in the middle of the huge open-plan office. After that, we were to decamp to their conference room to do the interview.

As The Girls checked their make-up once more, he disappeared for a minute, then returned saying he'd lead the way. We started to walk out of the small office into the open-plan area; looking round, I spotted the two girls who were featured on the front page of that day's paper being swept down the corridor towards us at considerable speed.

Panic bells started to ring inside my head. They would just happen to bump into us as we left the editor's office and they would, of course, photograph this historic meeting.

'Quick! Get back in that office!' I barked at The Girls. Shocked, but like little lambs taking it on the hoof from Old Shep, they belted back into the office a bit sharpish. I slammed the door shut behind them and, the adrenalin really pumping now, I yelled at Andy: 'We said NO, Andy!'

'All right, all right, calm down,' he snarled.

I walked into the office and closed the door behind me. 'Are you lot OK?' The Girls answered in the affirmative, and at once they bombarded me with questions.

'What's going on, Muff?'

'What the hell was that all about?'

'Are you OK, Muff?'

'I knew they were going to try something,' purred Geri.

I explained the situation and while The Girls were shocked by what had just happened, they were not surprised. 'Nothing would surprise me about these people,' Victoria said wryly.

We were interrupted by Coulson, sticking his head round the door.

'Can I have a word?' He gestured at me to go outside. 'Be careful, Muff,' shouted Mel B. Bless.

'That was totally unnecessary,' he whispered in my ear, while giving a glare that should have been defended with at least a Factor 20.

'What are you talking about, you've just tried to stitch us up!'

'No, we didn't. They were just coming up to say hello to Gary Bushell, that's all.'

'Yeah, right.'

'They were!'

'Andy, let's just agree to disagree on this one and get this finished. We'll skip the pictures out here and we'll just go into the conference room to do the interview. Who's doing the interview?'

'Dominic.'

'OK, but if there's anyone else in that conference room when we go in there, we walk!'

Tipping his head back, forcefully blowing the air out of his mouth, he echoed my last two words with emphatic, sarcastic disdain. I have not wanted a cigarette as much as I did then, since I gave up three years ago.

The interview with Dominic Mohan passed without incident, with The Girls quizzed on their TOP TEN SEXIEST MEN! among other topics.

Photo duties dispensed with, we started to make our departure.

We got into the cars and drove back to the main gate where The Girls posed as if arriving. As we went to leave, Mel B shouted out to Coulson who had joined us there: 'Bye, Andy! Nice try, Andy! You have to get up pretty early in the morning to catch us out, mate,' echoed by Geri's 'See ya! Wouldn't want to be ya!'

As my bottom hit leather in the car, we all heaved a collective sigh of relief. I passed round a bottle of Rescue Remedy and a mobile phone to call the other cars to make sure everyone was OK and to apologise about the wait until the next toilet-stop. Out of the three Jags speeding towards Elstree, I was sharing the back seat of one with Mel B, who was sitting next to me, next to her was Emma and in the front seat was Mel C.

As we drove we discussed the events of the past hour. Feelings ranged from disbelief and anger to a kind of necessitous, stoical resignation.

I explained that from now on the pressure from the newspapers would probably get worse and that they would probably start to approach their families and friends.

'They've already been in touch with some of my old school-friends,' said Melanie C.

'I know it goes with the territory,' said Emma, 'but it's bloody annoying, especially when they write stuff that's not true or when they try and pull a fast one like they did just now.'

'It's not as if we get the chance to say, now 'ang on a minute, that's not true, it's like this, is it?' added Melanie B. 'They don't give you the right to reply, do they?'

The talk turned to 'Kiss and Tell' stories and what the chances were that this behaviour was likely from their old boyfriends.

' 'Ow much do you think they'd get paid?' Melanie B asked.

'It depends on the story,' I replied. 'And also if they've got photos to go with the story. You could be talking anything from £2,000 to £10,000 – maybe much more. It all depends on the content.'

'Well, I can understand, if you've, say, been on the dole for four or five years and a paper turns up and offers you ten grand for your story, it's gonna be hard to turn that kind of money down isn't it? I understand, but I still wouldn't like it.'

As the conversation died away the car was filled with a poignant silence, as each of The Girls came to the sudden and graphic realisation that their lives were never, ever, going to be the same again.

Having hits is great, but when you become a (very) public figure there is a price to pay. Perhaps this was the moment when The Girls' armour started to form, when the last vestiges of innocence were wiped out or hidden away deep, deep down, away from the world, away from their conscious minds, to be replaced by hard shells, a necessary protection against the onslaught that would intensify and pursue them across the world in the coming year. Where was their personal refuge from the storm that was starting to squall around them?

It was almost as if The Girls aged on that journey from Wapping to the *Top of The Pops* studio. The Spice Girls would always be *The Girls!* but that day, something definitely shifted. They became women – older, wiser, yes; and happier? Who knows?

That night I slept very badly, enduring a fitful, sweaty slumber that was disturbed by a nightmare in which Andy Coulson appeared floating eerily above my bed, his face, covered in Day-Glo paint, hovering inches from mine. He leered like a madman, almost gurning while prodding me repeatedly in the chest. With a maniacal laugh he suddenly screamed: 'Welcome to the real world, Muff!' before disappearing as suddenly as he appeared.

Shaken, not to mention more than a little stirred-up by this unwelcome intrusion into my psyche, I pulled myself out of bed and staggered to the fridge to get a glass of soya milk. 'No Smoking!' my talking fridge magnet coughed and spluttered. After burning some incense to purify my bedroom and reciting the Vajrasattva Mantra, which is a protection against bad vibes, I eventually returned to the troubled arms of Morpheus.

The thing is Coulson's spectral self got it wrong. In the real world one knows what to expect. It was now that I inhabited

Spiceworld that I found perceptions changed, perspective shifted and the negative energies of paranoia and suspicion started to colour one's day-to-day decisions and inform one's judgement.

With Our Girls we had to be so careful. We had an agenda to adhere to, the trouble was the newspapers had their own agenda and from here on in they tried to hi-jack The Girls for their own purposes.

Virgin's agenda was quite straightforward: we wanted to make The Spice Girls one of the biggest pop acts in history. But in doing so we wanted to maintain their credibility and uphold their unique image. My role was as much about protection as promotion. I was devoted to The Girls and would do anything to see that no harm came to a single hair on each of their pretty heads.

After the incident at the *Sun*, I brought them into my daily morning meditation and prayer. My meditation practice was something that was going to sustain me throughout the crazy and demanding situations of the coming year.

During the Metta Bhavana, which is an expansive meditation designed to cultivate positive emotion and loving kindness, I asked that The Girls be well, happy and free from suffering. As I sealed my meditation with a few minutes' prayer, I asked Buddha and the powerful protectors, the Bodhisattvas, to look out for The Girls and to protect them from the unscrupulous attentions and unethical behaviour of the ladies and gentlemen from the tabloid press in particular, and anyone else with an axe to grind in general.

As a practising Buddhist, I spend my time trying to meet people on a human level and although this was sometimes quite difficult, as such it was always my intention to try to operate in a love mode as opposed to a power mode. Thrown into this maelstrom of aggression, bullying, deceit and general chicanery, I found it extremely stressful, not to say eye-opening and slightly disturbing.

However, I had to meet fire with fire, otherwise they would have walked all over me, and Our Girls. I was in for an intensive period of education, an education that continued with all the subtlety of the business end of a cattle prod.

The following morning, despite our less than ideal ordeal at Wapping, I was on the phone first thing to the *Sun*, to thank Andy and Dominic for our first front-page trailer and double-page feature. We did, after all, have to keep the lines of communication open. That's what PR is all about.

The next day all of us in Spiceworld were buzzing about a double-page feature in the *Independent* by Emma Forrest. In an enthusiastic piece she insisted that: 'This group could only have come about after seventeen years of Tory rule. There is a dash of yuppie, a dash of page-three girl to them. They are Essex girl incarnate, yet at the same time they are the band of the next government! The message is pull yourself up by your boot straps. And then pull everyone else up with you. Spice Girls *are* new Labour.'

A week later, Tony Blair chose 'Say You'll Be There' as one of his Top Ten records of the year for the *NME*.

Life in Spiceworld was punctuated with peaks and troughs, invariably on the same day. This would be one such day. In the real world, we all hate Mondays and look forward to Friday. In Spiceworld, Friday became a day to fear, for the simple reason it was usually around about five p.m. on a Friday that the Sunday tabloids would phone asking for comments on the sleazy stories they had prepared for that weekend's paper. I grew to loathe Fridays.

While still exuberant over the *Independent* story, the phone rang. It was a friendly freelance journalist who wrote for some of the tabloids. She told me she'd just heard that the *News of the World* had bought some nude photos of Geri which they were going to publish that weekend. About five minutes later I had a call from Sarah Stephens, who wrote for the *Sunday Sport*. Would I confirm the story that there were some nude photos of Geri in existence? Feigning ignorance, I said I had no idea and would have to call her back, which was my usual tactic to avoid commenting on an issue.

We had known about Geri's glamour modelling career for some months and knew it was just a matter of time before some of the pictures started to surface. That week, prior to the first publication, one of the photographers had seen Simon Fuller at 19 Management and asked for £40,000 for the negatives and a set of prints. Simon passed on the offer, pointing out that who knew how many sets of prints were already in circulation? As it transpired, such an action wouldn't have plugged all the holes in our leaky boat, which was to develop even more leaks over the next few days.

Geri had told us about her modelling career of which she was rather proud. It was something she'd done when she was seventeen, enjoyed the experience and had no regrets about. However, the full extent of her short-lived modelling career was yet to reveal itself to us.

Sarah Stephens called again. Would I please confirm that Geri had been a nude model? Knowing by now that the *News of the World* was definitely running their pictures on Sunday, I confirmed that Geri had made no secret of her nude modelling, and that she was proud of what she'd done.

Big mistake. I learned a valuable lesson there. In situations like these, it is prudent never to veer from those two golden words: no comment.

That Sunday, the *News of the World* ran a trailer on the front page that declared: 'Spice Girl's Nude Photo Shock', with a photo and story captioned 'Naughty But Spice' and said they thought these pictures would turn up shortly in some men's magazines 'but don't forget you cinnamon these pages first!'

The other Girls were not happy with Geri. It wasn't the nude modelling that upset them, it was the fact that Geri had not told them about the extent of her modelling career and had played down the number of sessions she'd done. The incident was used as an occasion to redistribute the dynamics of power within the group.

While on a promotional tour of Thailand The Girls had had a big row, after which Geri was treated coolly by the other Girls and was a shadow of her former self for a couple of months, when the cameras had been put away and the microphones switched off. The group's dynamic had shifted. It was probably also as much that Geri had been a very dominant force in the group until that point, and as the other Girls' confidence had grown they found they also wanted their own voices and opinions to be heard. They no longer needed a self-appointed spokeswoman. It was more of a democracy after this incident.

The same day the *Sun* first featured Geri's nude shots, they also ran a double-page spread on Emma's mum, Pauline, who had been door-stepped by a journalist and photographer at a church hall in East Finchley, where Pauline ran a karate class. Since she had used a photo of Emma (herself a green belt) to advertise the classes on a flyer, this intrusion was to be expected really.

That same week the *Daily Star* ran a story asking its readers: 'Who is the most famous 18-year-old in Britain, the *Daily Star*, or Emma Bunton?'

Sadly for the *Star*, it was not Emma, for Emma was in fact twenty years old. OK, so a few of The Girls had shaved a couple of years off their ages, but they were their 'pop' ages, as I kept telling people, after the *Sun* let the cat out of the bag a few days later, with great relish – having gone to the effort of tracking down Emma's birth certificate.

Opinion on this latest Spice Girls' outrage was divided. The day after the *Sun*'s 'exposé', the *Evening Standard* ran a sympathetic editorial which supported Emma's white lie: 'Next year, Emma should say she is seventeen. There is something bashful and becoming about lying about your age; it would be a tragedy if The Spice Girls lost that crucial touch of femininity.'

The *Daily Star* got their own back a few months later when Emma celebrated her twenty-first birthday at London's Atlantic club. The paparazzi were confined to the pavement outside, but the *Star* also had one of their reporters in the restaurant for a meal. She followed Mel C and Emma into the toilet and, without disclosing who she was, told them her nieces were their biggest fans and could she please have a photo of her with them. The Girls duly obliged and the following day the *Star* ran a front-page story with double-page feature inside which jubilantly crowed that they were the 'ONLY paper to be invited to Emma's birthday!' – and of course printed the picture of their reporter with Emma and Melanie as proof.

It was at this point, with The Girls fixed firmly as the object of the tabloids' attentions, that Simon Fuller took the unprecedented step of employing a libel and litigation expert. This action – virtually unknown in pop circles – was to prove very handy, indeed, not to mention reassuring, knowing that we had a hotshot lawyer as a back up, should things continue to snowball as they looked like doing.

Things were indeed hotting up, with the ex-boyfriends about to queue up to sell their stories. Gerrard Tyrell, a lawyer who had years of experience representing Hollywood actors and actresses, would go above the editors' heads to their senior management, informing them that if the papers printed mendacious stories about The Spice Girls then they would be sued and denied access to them from that moment on.

It was a strategy that at least made them think twice and slowed down the deluge of stories that were now becoming the nation's daily dose of Spice. Although there were still occasions when having an expert like Tyrell on our side still couldn't stem the tide – like the time when Emma's grandparents apparently gave photos of her as a baby to the *Mirror* along with their story.

The press were desperate for photographs of The Girls. Either current photos or photos from their lives before the group, or shots of their families. This was an area that we were quite successful at policing. Every photographer who took photographs of the group was required to sign a photo-release form which effectively said that The Spice Girls retained copyright and ownership of those images and that aside from the specified and mutually agreed publication date, any further reproduction of those images would require written permission from The Girls or their management.

Roughly half of my time was now spent enforcing these forms. I had become a fully sworn-in deputy of the Spice Police and as such it was my duty to enforce to the full letter of the law the terms outlined in these legal documents.

The reason behind this logic was simple. If you control the images of the group, then you have a much more effective control over the media who wish to use these photographs. If there aren't any photographs to accompany a story, then it puts you in a better bargaining position if you give permission to a paper to use a photo. You could, for instance, ask for copy approval on the feature that the photo is to accompany. Restrict the flow of photos and it can prove to be an effective regulator.

A prime example was a few months later when the *Sun* was doing an intrusive piece on Mel B which was meant to run for several days. We didn't want the story to run at all and, ironically enough, their picture desk were on the phone ten times a day, telling us they couldn't get hold of any pictures of her and could we let them have some? We politely and persistently refused and their two day 'exclusive' was whittled down to one day's coverage.

The other reason to keep a tight rein on the photos was to restrict the ever-increasing flood of pirated and unofficial merchandise, which was a multimillion pound industry.

Living in a gold-fish bowl, in the atmosphere of constant pursuit and intrusion, brought The Girls together and made them really close. It became them against the rest of the world. Victoria, Melanie C, Geri, Melanie B and Emma were like sisters and gave each other constant support. Of course, as mentioned, the dynamics changed all the time, but basically The Girls were as tight as a drum. They had to be.

Having been initiated into the realities of life as lived in Spiceworld, and firmly embarked on this rite of passage with fear, loathing and paranoia as our watchwords, things couldn't get any worse from here on in, could they?

Or could they?

Chapter Three

. . . .

THE ULTIMATE
TURN ON!

London, 7th November, 1996

'If you push a photographer out of the way, or manhandle him physically, then that can be classified as assault. So, there are little tricks you can use to get them out of the way and to make sure they don't get their shot.'

Jerry Judge, head of Music and Artists Security, was running us through his technique. 'As you come up to them you can "trip up" and go flying into them, and go "Oh, sorry, mate, are you all right? I just lost my footing there for a moment." Or you can come up and step on their feet "by accident". They can't do anything then. That's a good one.'

Jerry had been brought in to handle security for The Spice Girls. Because The Spice Girls were now more important than Jesus. We knew this because the *Independent On Sunday* said so. And also because in an hour from now they were due to switch on the Christmas lights in Oxford Street.

Jerry and his team handled The Girls' security at all public events from this point on. Jerry used to do the security for Take

That. He is a gentle giant, but someone who exudes authority and is more than capable of handling things if a situation turns nasty. And with Jerry around it never does. It's his job to see that it never does.

He's a solid bloke, one you'd trust your life with. And The Girls do. Daily. They adore him, with Scary going so far as to tell the *Daily Mirror*, when asked who her ideal man would be: 'Definitely Jerry Judge, he's a real man and a bit of a father figure. He'll die when he reads this!'

The only problem was, Jerry couldn't be with The Girls, or their families, the whole time. A couple of mornings earlier I'd received a distraught call from Victoria.

'Muff, can you do something please, I've just got up, I haven't got any make-up on, I've just gone down the road for a manicure and this photographer has followed me all the way from the house and he is waiting outside for me.'

I advised that she donned her sunglasses before leaving, smiled sweetly and then got out of there. Bloody paparazzi. I mean, a Girl can't even go and get her nails done now without being hassled, can she?

My advice to all of The Girls in such situations was always to smile and be very polite. If they were caught out and about on their own and if they felt like it and they had time, they could say to the papers 'Look, I'll pose for a quick photo for you if you'll leave me alone after that. OK?' Most of the time that worked. But there were the limpets who just stuck to them like glue, being totally intrusive and disturbing The Girls more than a little.

But The Girls were great, they were always polite, maintained their composure and basically learned to live with it. It was very important that they didn't lose their cool with those guys, because there's nothing the photographers – or the papers – love more than photos of an upset star, or even an upset star bashing a paparazzo.

But when it's their families being door-stepped and photographed, that's something else again. How do The Girls feel about it?

'I know that with me being a Spice Girl it brings with it certain responsibilities and pressures that are attached to the job. For instance the media,' informed an unhappy Melanie C. 'I know that goes with the territory, it's my job and it's a part of my job. But it's not my familiy's job and I think it's really unfair that they get hassled and harassed and put-upon so much. I think the media should just get a life.'

The pressure had been felt by all the families in the last few weeks. Melanie's little brother was followed home from school and photographed without his consent and all of the mums and dads had been door-stepped by journalists trying to persuade them to talk and to hand over personal photos. When this happened they referred the journalists to me. Either the mums passed on to me the journalists' numbers or they gave them mine and I would ask on behalf of the family for the journalist or photographer to respect their request for privacy and to leave them alone. They rarely complied and it became a constant battle to try and maintain any degree of privacy for any of The Girls and their families.

Eventually, we began to develop a siege mentality.

But right now in front of the Berkshire Hotel in Oxford Street, opposite the HMV store, The Spice Girls were being besieged by over five thousand screaming fans. And they were loving every minute of it.

'Are all those people down there waiting for us?' asked Scary, who was wearing a long brown coat that looked like a duvet cover. 'D'ya like my sleeping bag?' she then made a point of asking everyone.

'Listen, they're playing our music all the way down Oxford Street,' informed Baby, as the crowd took up the chorus of

'Wannabe' and ran with it like a gang of shoplifters taking it on their uppers.

Melanie C joined Emma at the window. A roar went up from the crowd. They had been spotted. They waved. A thousand tiny flashes like a distant constellation greeted the stars' gesture of acknowledgement, as some of the crowd tried to record the moment for posterity.

We were in the bedroom of a suite on the fifth floor of the Berkshire Hotel, while outside in the lounge were Simon Fuller, a throng of executives from Virgin, a camera crew, two competition winners and a photographer and journalist from the *Daily Mirror*, waiting to gain audience with The Girls.

That night after they had switched on the lights, there was the launch party for their album *Spice*. The album was released four days previously and today we had received the mid-week position for the album. Once again, it was the only number The Spice Girls understand: Numero Uno. Giving a double cause for celebration.

The Girls were buzzing. This was the first time they'd come into direct contact with their public and what a way to kick off.

For me, it was going to be a long night. Firstly, because at a public event you can never know 100 per cent what's going to happen. There may be an accident with some of the fans, there may be an incident with some of the press – you're always on edge and on your guard. The Girls' welfare is always the prime objective. If they're OK, then you're OK, despite being on edge with the adrenalin coursing through your body like Schumacher and Villeneuve on overdrive. And even though we'd got Jerry Judge and his men there, I was not able to relax for an instance, besides I'd got the *Daily Mirror* there, and they had to be looked after. Looked after *and* kept at a distance.

Which brings me to the other reason this was going to be a long night.

Because of the recent intrusions by the tabloid press, it had been decided that they were not welcome at that night's launch party, which was to be held at the OXO tower. Their reaction to this 'ban' (their word, not ours – they just weren't invited) had not been good.

The *Daily Mirror* with which our relationship had so far been a tad problematic, were particularly peeved. We had accommodated them with a photo shoot and a feature around the release of 'Say You'll Be There' but, due to an unavoidable turn of events, the *Sun* had run their story first and the *Daily Mirror* felt they'd been scooped and were understandably upset.

My daily contact (and boy, do I mean daily) was Matthew Wright, who was responsible for the Wright Stuff column ('If you're not in it, you're nobody!'). An intense rivalry exists between the *Mirror* and the *Sun*. The *Sun* is, of course, the market leader with probably three times as many sales. The *Mirror*, as the underdog, tends to fight harder for their 'showbiz' stories, with both Matthew Wright and Andy Coulson from the *Sun* referring to each other on their respective pages, in pantomime fashion, as 'my tired rival' or 'my sad rival'. Despite the vaudevillian way in which these put-downs arrived on the page, behind the scenes there was an intense and quite bitter rivalry between the two men.

Like Coulson, Wright is tarred with the same brush of unashamed tenacity, which is a prerequisite of any 'friend of the stars'. Once he gets his teeth into something, he will not let go. If Wright has the faintest whiff of a story he will call a hundred times a day. To say he is persistent is like saying the Pope is a Polish fella with a penchant for pointy hats. And behind Wright stands the shadow of his boss, the editor, Piers Morgan, who, incidentally, is best friends with Coulson from the time they worked together at the *Sun*. 'We make a point of never talking business, though,' Coulson once told me.

From around the end of October onwards, at least half of my

working day was spent fielding alternate calls from Wright and Coulson. I felt like the filling in a tabloid sandwich and these guys were doing their level best to wear me out.

It was extremely difficult to keep both papers happy all the time. In an ideal world, one would obviously like to see extensive coverage in both titles all the time, which isn't easy, but it was sometimes possible to put their rivalry and paranoia about each other to good use. Coulson's catch-phrase is 'You haven't done a deal with the *Mirror*?, Wright's turned out to be 'You've already given it to the *Sun*, haven't you?' or just as often: 'The boss is not happy!'

From around this time, we could never discuss work in public for fear of being overheard and bubbled to the tabloids. Everyone, right down to the postman, builder, estate agents, airline and hotel clerks were on an earner. We couldn't talk about our plans over the phone after BT investigated and found out that Geri's land-line was being tapped. We suspected a national newspaper. Mobile phones were also a no-no, unless they were digital and couldn't be scanned.

Sometimes it felt as though the British tabloid press had better resources and a bigger success rate than the Thought Police and The Met put together.

So that evening at the hotel on Oxford Street, we had present the *Daily Mirror* and the two competition winners, Zoë Page and Holly Gramlick, who had won a phone-in competition to come and meet The Girls and watch them switch on the lights. The *Mirror* had promised us a page one lead with the competition but, because they were not invited to the party, they punished us by burying the offer in a tiny paragraph on page nine.

Before The Girls went down to their convoy of Jags, with attendent police escort, I took Zoë and Holly to meet The Girls and to get their photo taken with them by John Ferguson, the *Mirror*'s photographer.

The Girls were all over them.

'Hiya!'

'Oh, thanks for coming to meet us!'

'Have you got the album yet? No? Oh Muff, you must get them both a copy of the album!'

'Yeah, we can't believe it either, turning on the Oxford Street lights, what an honour.'

'Of course you can have our autographs. Muff, have you got a pen, please?'

After picture and signing duties were dispensed with and I'd taken Zoë and Holly and company to the hospitality room, I went back upstairs.

The Girls wanted a bit of space.

'Muff, can you make sure no one comes in for five minutes please,' asked Emma. They just needed to chill, focus and collect themselves before going out to greet the huge crowd who had sealed off Oxford Street.

After a few minutes they were ready. Jerry Judge took them downstairs and after posing for another photo with Zoë and Holly as they get into their cars, they were driven round the block with police motorcycles in tow, blue lights flashing in delirious counterpoint to the flashing of thousands of cameras that were scattered from the press pit right through the swollen ranks of the screaming crowd.

As The Girls ascended the cherry-picker where the Lord Mayor of London and Dr Fox, the DJ from Capital Radio, greeted them, their faces were flushed and beatific. They were completely overwhelmed by the occasion and the enthusiastic response from the crowd.

'I just want to say a big thank you to all our fans,' screamed Geri, adding a V-sign, 'Girl Power!'

'Yeah, it's great to be here, I just want to say thank you,' echoed Victoria.

'Hello Mum!' shouted Emma, giving her mum, Pauline, a little wave.

Then it was the countdown.

'T-E-N!'

'N-I-N-E!'

'E-I-G-H-T!'

'S-E-V-E-N'

'S-I-X!'

F-I-V-E faces that were filled with the biggest grins of their lives. Five women who had just realised how MASSIVE they actually were, the effect they have had on people's lives and the full extent of their new found popularity. Forget all the hassle and intrusion from the tabloids, it was moments like this that put everything into perspective, moments like this that made all the hard work, the eighteen-hour days, the months away from home and loved ones, the relentless pursuit by paparazzi, the endless hours of hair and make-up, actually worth it.

They realised then, just how famous they were. The Girls were buzzing. They had truly arrived. Girl Power! was here to stay!

'F-O-U-R!'

'T-H-R-E-E!'

'T-W-O!'

'O-N-E!'

They hit the button on the Sony Play Station and Oxford Street lit up like a four-year-old's face on Christmas Morning. But that was nothing as to how The Girls' faces were lit up. They were ecstatic.

They ran down the steps of the cherry-picker and did a lap of honour around the edges of the crush barriers, dispensing autographs, handshakes and kisses. They were literally bouncing up and down with joy. Geri grabbed a small boy who had climbed over the barrier, hoisted him over her shoulder and ran away with him down the street. From the press pit a hundred motor-drives were turning over, the staccato effect of their flash-guns making Geri dance gaily under a non-stop strobe-light.

Today was the best day of their lives. (So far.)

Having to be virtually carried back into their cars and restrained, The Girls were then taken to a reception at Debenhams, where they met the families of the Oxford Street Association which had organised the event and invited The Girls to perform the lighting up duties.

'I wanted to stay there all night,' Victoria said as we walked in.

'It was such a mad buzz,' gushed Melanie B.

Geri, unsurprisingly, was in agreement. 'I loved it. They loved us didn't they?'

After that they went off for a couple of hours to chill out with their families, while I headed straight for the OXO tower where I would be standing by the door for most of the night checking the press guest-list.

The launch party was really an industry function, as opposed to a star-studded celebrity bash. The object of such a launch is to invite all the main movers and shakers from the world of television, radio and press, those who've been supportive so far and those whose help we would need in supporting the band in the future.

Halfway through the evening there would be a gigantic firework display, which cost £65,000 to stage. To enable this event to go ahead, the Metropolitan River Police had closed off the Thames for an hour.

At our weekly Spice Planning Meeting a few weeks before, when we were organising the launch, it was suggested that The Girls perform 'Wannabe' standing on Tower Bridge, before the party, with a fleet of helicopters filming the event for inclusion in The Girls' video. Sadly, this idea never got past the planning stage, but we would have some fun and games with a helicopter some months later when we set up a photo shoot on top of the Empire State Building in New York.

At that same meeting, we also discussed the now real possibility that the 'Dunblane' single was a strong contender for the Christmas Number One slot.

This was obviously an extremely sensitive issue and needed to be handled delicately, to say the least. Melanie C had already gone on record as saying: 'We'll be releasing a Christmas single, which we'd love to get to Number One. But if anybody is going to beat us, we'd love it to be the children of Dunblane. We'll be buying copies.'

That summed up The Girls' feelings on the matter. It was decided to put the release date of '2 Becomes 1' back a week, to give the 'Dunblane' single, 'Knocking On Heaven's Door', the chance of going to Number One, which looked set to be a certainty. That way we would hopefully take the spot the following week, with most people having bought their copies of 'Knocking On Heaven's Door' in the first week.

Back at the party, quite early on in the evening, I was standing at the entrance upstairs when Dominic Mohan, Andy Coulson's colleague from the *Sun*, walked by.

'Oh 'allo, Dominic,' I absent-mindedly greeted him.

'All right, Muff,' he responded.

'Dominic?' I then exclaimed out loud. 'Dominic, what are you doing here?'

'What do you mean?' he countered.

'Dom, you know you aren't invited, no tabloid journalists have been invited, mate.'

'Look, I'm just here with my mates, out to have a drink and a good night out.'

'Look Dom, could you wait here a minute, please.'

I asked the security guard who was standing by the entrance to 'keep this gentleman here for a minute, please' and I dashed off to let my boss Robert Sandall know. Robert was in discussion with some journalists at the bar. I took him aside.

'Robert, Dominic's here from the *Sun*.'

'Oh shit,' said Robert.

'What are we going to do?'

'Hmm, now calm down, Muff,' he said, with his characteristically charming and unflappable nature, noticing my ever-so-slightly hyper-ventilated state.

'Right, who's he here with?'

'He just arrived with Dominic Smith the editor from *Big!* and the *Big!* posse. He says he's just come for a drink and a night out.'

'Well, Simon doesn't want anyone from the tabloids in here tonight. This is Simon's edict, and we have to uphold it. If we are civilised and let him in "just to have a drink", firstly one of The Girls will recognise him and tell Simon—'

'And Simon will go spare!'

'Quite, and you can bet your life that tomorrow there will be a crowing "WE CRASHED THE SPICE GIRLS' PARTY!" piece in the Bizarre column.'

Robert paused for thought.

'Hmm, there's nothing else for it, Muffet, *you'll* have to ask him to leave.'

I gulped. 'You want me to throw the *Sun* out of the party?'

'That's about the size of it. Look, there's nothing else we can do.'

'Are you going to come with me?' I asked imploringly, like a five-year-old begging his dad to accompany him to school because he's scared of getting trounced by the school bully.

'Oh no, Muffet, I don't want to talk to these people, I think you're quite capable of handling the situation by yourself, now off you go . . .'

Back at the front door, I was as apologetic as I could be, but

Dom was not happy. When Andy Coulson rings the office, he's tense.

Dominic is actually quite an affable bloke, the sort of chap you could spend a pleasant evening down the boozer with. He never threatens or hectors, though he is persistent in his own way. And sometimes he's very funny. In a few months' time he will be the man who writes the 'GERI RUSHED TO HOSPITAL!' – turn to page five – 'TO HAVE A FINGERNAIL REMOVED FROM HER EAR' story. But he is a tabloid journalist after all, and at the back of my mind, there was always the nagging suspicion that he would never let a little thing like friendship get in the way of a story.

Like Coulson, his guv'nor, he is a newspaperman through and through.

'Look, I'm really sorry, Dom, but this isn't down to me.'

'Look, I only want to stay for a couple of drinks.'

'I'm sorry, mate.'

'Look, I've got a ticket.'

'I know, mate, but it wasn't sent to you, sorry.'

'Look, no one will know I'm here.'

'That's not the point, mate. Look, this isn't down to The Girls, they really like you, they really enjoyed the interview with you the other day. It's just a management decision. I'm really sorry, mate.'

After five more minutes of this exchange, which seemed like hours, we reached the denouement.

'Right, so you're definitely not going to let me in then?'

'I'm so sorry, mate,' I answered, feeling like I'm sympathising with someone over a bereavement. And I am. It's going to be my funeral after this incident, after all.

'All right, I'll go then,' he shouted angrily.

Turning his head round as the rest of his body makes for the door, he screamed. 'You know this means WAR! don't you?'

'Hello, Brown Eye!'

At the reindeer farm in Lapland, December 1996.

Posh and Sporty hit the snowmobiles.

With the Girls in Lapland,
my stylist not present.

Main picture and left: On top of the Empire State Building, New York, January 1997.

Above: Onstage at the Hialeah Festival, Miami, January 1997.

Main picture: The Girls with Dawn French, Jennifer Saunders, Kathy Burke, Lulu and Llewella Gideon at the "Who Do You Think You Are" video.

Opposite, clockwise from top left: Baby and Posh; Jennifer Saunders does a Ginger!; Dawn French and Posh.

The Girls being interviewed by Andy Coulson in New Orleans, St Valentine's Day, 1997.

Onstage at the Gavin Radio Convention in New Orleans, being presented with discs to commemorate going to Number One in America with "Wannabe". St Valentine's Day, 1997.

Reaching for my Rescue Remedy, I took a quick swig then made immediately for the bar, where I dispatched a large, neat vodka.

The Girls arrived about an hour later and the incident passed without further event. Or maybe that should be the other way round. Or maybe not.

We were door-stepped by a reporter from the *Evening Standard*, who had heard that a child got hurt in the crush at the lights ceremony, and he was following up a rumour that the child was more distressed at missing out on the opportunity of getting her album signed. Apparently, Victoria's mum, Jacqui, comforted the child and promised to send her the group's autographs. He promised he'd leave as soon as he got a quote.

I got hold of Victoria and she said she didn't mind having a quick word with him. I told her that if he started to ask her about anything else then just to say she had to go and hand the phone back to me. She told him that 'Yes, my mum, did help a girl who'd fallen over and she took her name and address and promised to send her a signed photograph.'

Although it was The Girls' party, they couldn't relax. They were there to work and I took them around to meet the various editors and features editors who had been responsible for commissioning the articles that had been running since I started working on their campaign; while Nick Godwyn and Nikki Chapman introduced The Girls respectively to the grand fromage's from the world of television and radio.

Finally, at around midnight, we got The Girls together for a quick photo by a fridge filled with champagne and then we got them in to their Jags. It had been quite a day for everyone and one hell of a week.

*   *   *

Two days before, The Girls had been shooting the video for '2 Becomes I' at Tower Bridge Studios in London. On the first day of shooting I brought along journalist Paul Moody, who was writing a cover story for the following week's *NME*. Being at a video shoot is not quite as glamorous as most people think. It's an extremely long haul – eighteen- and twenty-hour days being the norm, with a horrendous amount of waiting around, punctuated by a few minutes of excessively frantic activity every now and again.

The Girls were portrayed against a blue screen with footage shot in New York the week before, cleverly superimposed to make it look like they were in that city's gorgeous winterland. I felt I'd achieved a minor victory a few weeks later when the *Sun* ran a story saying New York had been brought to a standstill as The Girls caused traffic chaos when they were winched up into the rafters of the Brooklyn Bridge for their new video.

Getting the cover of the *NME* was a real milestone for The Girls – it totally surprised a lot of people and was extremely valuable in broadening the ever growing 'Church of Spice'. However, at the time, in spite of assurances from Mark Sutherland, the features editor, that it was not their intention to perform a stitch-up, I was a little on edge. I would have been an idiot not to be.

When Paul Moody walked in unannounced he caught me having an intense conversation with Melanie B. Her mum had just been door-stepped by the *Daily Star* and they'd offered her £2,000 (a rather insulting fee, actually) to give them a story. A little later, I would call Andrea and advise her about what to do and say when pestered by journalists at home. However, a few weeks later she decided to let a journalist from the *Sun* into her house and gave them an interview to get them off her back.

After introducing Paul to everyone, at the next break point I gathered all The Girls into a dressing room and they started their interview. I got the feeling Paul was a little overwhelmed, outnumbered five to one, (as Jim Morrison sang: five to one baby, one in five, no one here gets out alive!).

About half an hour later, Geri came out of the cramped room to get a drink. 'Oh, Muff, he's wicked! He's really mad. You bring all the best people down to talk to us don't you?'

'Oh thank you, Geri,' I replied, pleased that she was having a good time, but at the same time I was a little concerned about Geri's exuberance. I felt extremely protective of her because of all the nude shots that had appeared in the press during the past few weeks. Despite her honest statement that she was proud of what she did, it had been an enormous thing to have to deal with. She must have been feeling extremely exposed psychologically, as well as the obvious physical exposure, and she had coped admirably, but I did worry about her and felt for her deeply.

I was worried that with her trusting nature she might start gushing to Paul, who might put an adverse spin on her candid and enthusiastic conversation.

I tried to dampen her down a little. 'That's brilliant. I'm really glad you like him, but still be careful, won't you? They're not down here to do a stitch up, but I'd advise a bit of caution.'

'Oh,' said Geri, deflated, her smile disappearing and looking a trifle paranoid now, I could almost see her mind quickly rewinding the previous half hour, checking herself to see what she'd already told him.

This made me feel bad, for while wanting to steer her away from any impetuosity, I didn't want to lower her spirits in any way.

I was also feeling quite protective of Geri because of the recent row among The Girls and the shift in the group's dynamic.

When The Girls had come back from a promo tour in Thailand, Geri was a shadow of her former self. It was quite shocking to see. Away from the cameras and microphones, the girl who was normally the most shouty member had begun acting like a church mouse. Perhaps she'd needed this vociferous exchange of views, perhaps she had dominated for too long and the other Girls needed to express themselves but, even so, the change in her had moved me quite deeply and I felt concerned for her. I wanted to help her, I felt she'd had a hell of a lot on her plate lately and in the situation she was in, who could she turn to?

In my role as PR, I always tried to be as supportive as possible but, ultimately, the strength has to come from within. I'd given Geri a book on Buddhism and some tapes that take one through a led meditation. As Geri already possessed an enthusiastic pioneering spirit along the self-help trail and was always to be spotted clutching either a psychological or spiritual tome, I thought she might be interested and that these may be of some help.

The group interview concluded, though Paul Moody wanted to interview them individually as well. As The Girls did their solo parts for the video, I took whoever was not being filmed in to talk with Paul.

At this stage in the game, we were all still on a learning curve. The Girls were learning what not to say in interviews, and also that what they said to a friendly journalist from the music press while they were feeling relaxed and off-guard would end up in print and would be used against them by the tabloid press: they were finding out the hard way all of the things that had to be taken on board to enable them to cope with their new found celebrity.

Celebrity is like an extremely expensive overcoat. Once you try it on, if it fits, you then have to watch your back the whole time. There's always some sharp so-and-so intent on either relieving you of it, or running to the papers to talk about the night you made love in it while wearing nothing else in front of a roaring log fire.

I sat in with each girl, reading a magazine in the corner and making sure the journalist didn't try to lead them on any taboo topics, such as politics, for instance.

During Geri's interview he asked her if she'd ever been arrested? I expected her to just say NO! But she said, rather earnestly, 'I'd rather not comment on that.' Geri and Mel B were once arrested while on holiday for drunkenness in Gran Canaria, but the cops didn't take them down to the police station, but changed their minds and let them go.

In the light of all the recent tabloid shenanigans, when I was alone with Paul a little later on I asked him not to print anything to do with that question and Geri's reply.

'Paul, The Girls have been through hell over the last few weeks, particularly Geri. The tabloids have really got it in for them and if you print that, they're going to pick up on it and it's going to cause even more problems for Geri. Please don't print it, mate?'

'Well, yeah, all right man, yeah, errr, like yeah man, I'll see what I can do . . .' he said with not enough conviction or confirmation in his voice for my liking.

Sure enough, the following week he'd printed the question and the response; he's a journalist, so what did I expect?

During this long-drawn-out day that wouldn't end for The Girls until three in the morning, we still had to fit in the cover shoot for the *NME* and a five-minute film for MTV, which was to advertise a competition to take 170 children to Lapland to meet Father Christmas with The Spice Girls in December.

Carole Burton-Fairbrother, head of video at Virgin, who was responsible for organising the very tight and expensive schedule, decided that we would have to shoot both in the half an hour that The Girls had scheduled for their dinner break at eight thirty that evening. During that half-hour, the video crew would clear the set to film the baby deer, which was to appear at the end of the '2 Become 1' video.

It was probably the quickest photo shoot in history. We decamped to a studio we'd booked round the corner, with the MTV people getting fifteen minutes to do their bit and us fifteen minutes to shoot a cover and photos for the accompanying feature.

'Could someone please put in a call to Norris McWhirter, this is another one for the record books,' I joked. The Girls liked the speed of it though. If a photo session started to drag on and The Girls want the photographer to get a move on, it was one of their party pieces to start stamping their feet in time, together screaming out the intro to Gary Glitter's 'D'Ya Wanna Be In My Gang?': 'COME ON, COME ON, COME ON, COME ON, COME ON COME ON, C-O-M-E O-N!' The Girls don't like people faffing around when they're ready to rock. Although it's a bit of a different story when the platformed Buffalo shoe is on the other foot.

Around half The Spice Girls' waking hours are spent in hair and make-up. When they go on a photo shoot, have a television appearance to make, or are attending an awards ceremony or public function, they have to look their best, and looking good and feeling great can take a Girl some time.

There is a regular pool of hair and make-up artists The Girls use whom they have come to trust and rely on and who accompany them on all their engagements.

When you organise a photo shoot with The Spice Girls it's like planning a military campaign. There is a lot to organise. When you see The Girls glancing down at you from the cover of yet another glossy magazine, few people realise that the talent of about twenty skilled people is required to make that photograph happen.

Setting up a session involves booking a photographer and a

studio, lights and equipment and hair and make-up artists. Quite often with The Girls we used two people for hair and two for make-up, because with five Girls it can take quite a while. The Girls' cars then need to be booked to collect them, their stylist has to be contacted and put in touch with the photographer to discuss what the shoot will entail – the stylist keeps contact between The Girls and photographer – management, of course, need to be kept informed of all developments and as well as confirming everything with Simon Fuller, I would go over the minutiae with Camilla Howarth and Rachel Pinfold, The Girls' personal assistants.

I was always the first to arrive at a photo session and the last to leave. This was to make sure that everything was all right and to go and collect the food and drink that The Girls liked. I would always find out where the nearest supermarket was and go and do the shopping.

The Girls dietary habits are very healthy, they like to eat a lot of fresh fruit and raw vegetables. They drink an ocean of sparkling mineral water, but Victoria and Emma are very partial to Diet Coke. When they signed their deal with Pepsi, they found it quite difficult to remember to ask for Diet Pepsi and actually weren't terribly fond of it at all.

Victoria and Melanie C are very fond of fresh dates as well. As Victoria pointed out to me on my first culinary foray, 'They've got to be fresh, Muff, not the ones with the vegetable oil in, just fresh.'

If we were going to be at a studio all day or during a meal time, I would go out and buy lunch or dinner for everyone.

Melanie B loves chicken, rice and peas, which could sometimes be quite difficult to obtain if there wasn't a soul food restaurant in the vicinity. Failing that, she loves sausage, mash and onions, whereas Melanie C is very fond of sushi and steamed fish. Melanie C is the most health-conscious of all The Girls and was always turning up with vitamin supplements and herbal tonics, which help to keep her perfect body in shape. All The Girls have to stay in good health with their punishing schedule. There's no time to be sick when every day for the next year has already been plotted out.

Emma is fond of quite traditional food, such as Spaghetti Bolognaise or a roast dinner with two veg, while Geri likes healthy food such as salads or something with garlic in it. Victoria seems to live on a perpetual diet of steamed vegetables with balsamic vinegar – and absolutely no oil in the dressing, just balsamic vinegar. She also likes to eat a lot of fresh fruit.

If a shoot carried on into the evening, I would then procure drinks for everybody. All The Girls are partial to a glass of wine, while Victoria likes a gin and tonic, especially if she's wearing clear varnish. Being a real lay-dee, she quite often liked to co-ordinate her drink with the colour of her nail varnish.

Melanie B, and Emma like vodka and tonic, while Geri will occasionally go for something a little exotic, just like herself, ordering a crème de menthe or Drambuie.

When it came down to the thousands of hours they spent having their hair and make-up done, Melanie C was usually ready first and often volunteered to get her session out of the way. Victoria then took the next least time, then Emma, then Geri then Melanie B.

Geri and Melanie B took the longest to get ready because their hair is longer than all the others and therefore takes longer to prepare. However, Geri was famous for being longer than all the other Girls put together, due to her habit of deciding to try a new hairstyle at the last minute – much to the chagrin of the other Girls on occasion.

'Muff, can you go and tell Geri we're waiting for her,'

Melanie C said to me on more than one occasion. And if Geri took ages, then something else would always happen just as we were finally ready, after sitting round for three hours while lotions were applied, brushes swept through the air like conductors' batons and a few more acres of the ozone layer were turned to Gorgonzola due to the clouds of hairspray that hovered in the atmosphere like LA on a bad day (or is that a bad hair day?). Just as we'd get down to the video set/photo backdrop, either Melanie B or Geri, (usually Melanie B) would suddenly announce, 'Ooh, 'ang on a minute, I think I just need another bit of lippy!' and she would dash back to the dressing room to apply another layer of Cherry Erotique.

'Blimmin' heck!' would be Melanie C's response. She just hates faffing around.

When we were leaving a venue to get into the three Jags, I and the drivers (from the company Music Express, who had the contract to drive The Girls for the first year) would always make sure there were no paparazzi lurking. There always were though. The drivers, who acted as unofficial security when Jerry Judge wasn't around, would bring the cars round and try to ensure a swift and hassle-free departure for our glamorous charges.

But this could make what should have been a simple matter of leaving a building and getting into a car, a major operation. The drivers would communicate with each other by mobile phone, bring the cars round, we would line The Girls up by the door and then it was: 'GO, GO, GO!' as though The Girls were parachuting out of a plane or something.

While they were bringing the cars round and double-checking, Melanie C would sometimes get quite exasperated: 'Can we just go please!'

Looking round at me, she would say, 'I hate all this messing around, why can't we go and just get on with it?'

It was a pain, and having to behave like this day in and day out it must become very tedious. But it can be quite exciting too.

When you're with The Spice Girls, even the most mundane things become imbued with a great deal of drama. Nothing is ever as straightforward as it should be, everything can, and usually does, become problematic.

Two days after the launch party, I escorted Gavin Reeve, the charming editor of *Smash Hits*, and photographer Adrian Green to Paris to shoot the cover for the *Smash Hits* poll winners issue.

Originally they'd asked for The Spice Girls to share a cover with Boyzone, who were the other major award winners at that year's ceremony. We said no because we didn't want The Girls to be seen endorsing Boyzone. The way we saw it, they had a lot more to gain from the kudos of sharing a cover with Our Girls. We maintained our position and for the first time in its history *Smash Hits* produced an issue with a double cover – one with Boyzone and one with our Fab Five.

Because of The Girls' hectic schedule, we had to go to Paris to perform the shoot. The Girls were in Paris that day doing a shoot for the French edition of *Elle*. After they had finished, they were to drive across Paris to the rue des Acacias, to another studio we had booked, where we had an hour to shoot the cover, before they were to be driven to the airport to fly to New York for the first time. I was to meet them there the next day with Peter Lorraine, the editor of *Top Of The Pops* magazine.

On arrival in Paris, I dropped Gavin and Adrian off at the studio and drove over to the *Elle* studio to make sure we were running to schedule. Everything was going swimmingly.

I got a cab back to our studio and found the nearest super-market to buy some Perrier and Diet Cola. The Girls were on good form when they arrived. They love doing teen press, because they can relax since there are no hidden agendas. They were all quite excited about going to New York as well. On top of that, they had all just booked Christmas holidays in the Caribbean.

All The Girls were looking forward to their holidays enormously, having worked so hard for the last nine months, slogging their guts out eighteen hours a day, with very few days off. I warned them to be on their guard against photographers when they were on holiday. The papers would pay top dollar for pictures of The Girls topless on the beach, and the paparazzi would be on their trail.

'I'm keeping my top on,' said Emma.

Melanie B declared, 'I'm not bothered; if they want to take a picture of me, they can.'

'Ooh no,' said Victoria, 'I'm definitely keeping my top on.'

I asked who they were going with.

Melanie B was going to visit relations. Geri was going with a friend, Victoria was going with Stuart, her boyfriend. Mel C was taking her family out there. And Emma was taking her mum Pauline, her brother Paul and boyfriend, Mark. Emma said she'd booked a package job in a three-star hotel in Barbados.

When Emma told me that, I was worried, because I was sure she was going to get the most hassle. It's sadly true in life, that you get what you pay for. Her celebrity status had left her marked down for endless intrusion and as such, sadly, she should have kept to the confines of a more exclusive hotel, which protects its guests, or rented a private villa.

She looked crestfallen. I didn't mean to burst her bubble, but perhaps there was still time to change her booking. In the event, deciding not to, she just went and hoped for the best.

Our managing director at Virgin, Paul Conroy, who was also going to Barbados for Christmas, had kindly extended an invitation to Emma and her family for them to hang out at his more exclusive hotel, where invasions of privacy were not tolerated. She declined his offer. You want to get away from work completely when you go on holiday, don't you?

Consequently, on 9 January the papers were full of photographs of Emma and her mum, and Emma kissing her boyfriend Mark Verquese. The *Daily Mail* were particularly nasty. On the front page they had printed a photograph of Emma and Pauline in their swimsuits, taken from behind, stating here is a Spice Girl and her mum and snidely asking whether readers could tell them apart?

It backfired on the *Mail*, and they had their biggest ever mailbag from outraged women across the country, demanding to know what was wrong with having a normal, healthy figure.

It was one of those occasions when I felt impotent and unable to help much. The photographer in question had taken the room directly opposite Emma and Pauline's and was on their trail every step of the way. I kept phoning his room to ask him to desist from hassling them both, but he never answered the phone. Quite appallingly, the hotel management refused to throw him out.

And Emma and Pauline? Pauline said to me when she got back: 'We were devastated by it. We just lay in bed all day crying and holding on to each other, trying to comfort each other. I've never felt so bad about anything in my life. It was so horrible.'

Just before The Girls left the *Smash Hits* shoot, Melanie C asked how my tattoo was getting on – I'd had four colours filled in so far and it was starting to take shape.

'That's really coming on now, Muff, it looks really painful though.'

'Ooh yes Muff, that's really swollen isn't it,' said Victoria. I'd only had it done the evening before and as the process is somewhat similar to putting your arm in a sewing machine, it leaves you quite swollen and scabby for about a week afterwards.

Victoria had a rummage around in her bag and pulled out a jar of ointment.

'Listen Muff, this is the stuff they use for putting on rashes on babies' bottoms. I use it on my face, because it gets quite sore with having to put make-up on and off four times a day. I think it will really help to heal it.'

'Aaah, thanks, Vic,' I responded, touched.

'That's all right, Muff,' she said sweetly, while gently applying the cream to the afflicted area. 'You look after us, Muff, so we have to look after you.'

I was deeply moved by this loving gesture.

After The Girls had departed, Gavin, Adrian and I morosely packed up the equipment. It felt like we'd suffered a loss.

'It always feels like this after The Girls have gone doesn't it?' said Gavin.

'Yeah, it does,' I replied, 'I know exactly what you mean, Gav.'

'It's sort of sad, isn't it?' he continued. 'It's quite depressing when they've left isn't it, they're just . . . oh, they're great, aren't they?'

'Yeah, they are mate, they're FAB!'

To cheer us all up I took Gavin and Adrian out for a slap-up feast at La Coupole, haunt of Ernest Hemingway and a must-visit on any trip to Paris. This was one of the great perks of my job, eating at the best restaurants and seeing the world at someone else's expense(s)!

The next morning I got up at six to fly back to Heathrow where I was to meet Peter Lorraine and photographer Julian Barton to fly to New York.

We arrived after a leisurely flight spent reading the Sunday papers. The *Sunday Mirror* had tracked down the 'sixth' Spice Girl, Michelle Stephenson, who was one of the original five but who left to go to university. Meanwhile, the *News of the World* had printed a photo of Melanie B with an ex-boyfriend, Julian Bennett, who had just pleaded guilty to smuggling sixty kilos of hashish into the country. While the *News of the World* stated that: 'There is no suggestion that Mel knew anything about the smuggling,' there was a ridiculous claim from 'friends' that he did it to try and keep up with her lifestyle.

Mel hadn't even seen him for five years, and it was Bennett's sister, Debbie, who went to the papers while he was in prison and sold them the picture of them together, which apparently he was livid about.

There was some good news that day though. As predicted, the album *Spice*, about which *The Times* said '[it] has a depth of feeling that goes well beyond the superficial charm of traditional teen pop', had gone straight to Number One, outselling the other top five albums by four to one.

We caught up with The Girls at the Royalton Hotel at ten a.m. on Monday morning. Their spirits were high. They were really pleased to be in New York for the first time and over the moon that *Spice* had gone to Number One.

While The Girls began their first interview with *DJ Times* in Melanie C's room, I went to change some money for The Girls, because as everybody knows, when the going gets tough, the tough go shopping!

On my return, while sitting downstairs in the lobby with Peter and Julian, we were joined by Suzanne Macnarry and Yon Elvira from the Virgin America press office and a woman called Susan Blond, an independent PR, and her assistant. Susan had been handling some of the specialist dance press and used to be a close friend of Andy Warhol's, hanging out on The Factory scene and appearing naked in one of his films.

Peter, Julian and I were discussing where we wanted to shoot The Girls for *Top Of The Pops* magazine. They were producing a sixteen-page poster book, and needed to shoot at various locations. Julian wanted to take some shots of The Girls in Time Square and was talking about shooting them in the middle of the crossing, just after the lights had gone green so we could do a 'Spice Girls Bring New York To A Standstill'-type shot.

Suzanne didn't think this was such a good idea.

'No, I really don't think you should do that. They won't stop for you, you know. Those taxi drivers will try and run you down.'

'That's right, you know,' piped in Susan Blond's assistant, adding in pure Noo Yawk, 'she's totally not kidding!'

Peter and I exchanged glances, trying to stifle our laughter.

'She's totally not kidding,' became our catch-phrase for the rest of the jaunt. Although we added 'already' on the end for extra effect.

'I'm totally not kidding about this, already,' was my new mantra, delivered in a falsetto nasal whine. I love New York.

We went shopping. Peter and Julian travelled in the Previa with Geri, Victoria, Melanie B and Melanie C, while behind, I travelled in the stretch-limo with Emma, Simon Fuller and Joe Dyer, top bloke and ace cameraman, who was shooting *Spice – The Video*.

First stop Macy's. On the way there I started going on about the Tommy Hilfiger stuff I'd bought on previous trips to New York and that I wanted to buy a puffa jacket on this trip. Simon said that Tommy Hilfiger had expressed an interest in doing something with The Girls, and asked me what I thought of his stuff.

'It's the best!' I replied. 'It's good quality sportswear, and he's at that stage in crediblity terms that Calvin Klein was, say five years ago. And the other thing about Hilfiger stuff is that you can't buy it in Britain yet, so there's that exclusive element attached to it.'

Simon flicked through his Psion organiser, but he'd left the number for Andy Hilfiger, who handled PR for Tommy, in London.

I borrowed Simon's mobile phone and obtained the number for Hilfiger's head office, who then gave me Andy Hilfiger's number.

'Oh, hello, this is Simon Fuller's personal assistant. Simon is the manager of the chart-topping Spice Girls who are currently Number One in twenty-seven countries around the world. We understand that Tommy is interested in doing something with The Girls and Simon would like to discuss this with Andy. I have Simon on line now for Andy . . . Oh, he's not there right now, could I leave this number and have him call? Thank you . . .'

'That was very good, Muff,' said Simon, 'I think you'd make a very good PA.'

At Macy's, everyone wanted to buy different things so we all split up with an arrangement to meet back at the rear entrance in one hour. I went with Simon and Emma to the male Designer underwear section. Simon and I wanted to buy some pants.

It is a veritable Aladdin's cave of boxers, jockeys and briefs. We wandered round with our baskets, which were filled quite quickly, though Simon was buying four to my one.

'What do you think of these, mate?' he asked Emma, holding up a knee-length pair of multicoloured Hilfiger pants. He called everone mate, including all The Girls.

'They're funny,' replied Emma smiling.

'Yeah, I suppose if one's seduction technique was wavering a bit, then these could supply a comedy effect,' he laughed, putting them in his basket.

I put a pair in my basket too. After banging on so much about Hilfiger, I figured I had to put my credit card where my mouth was, and also, I was busy trying to keep up with Simon in the basket-filling stakes. I shouldn't have. He was a millionaire. I was not.

When we finally took our baskets to the cash desk, I was staggered. My bill was $357.16 cents, including tax. Well knock me down with a small piece of plastic. I'd just spent over £200 on underpants. What an idiot. I mean how many pairs of pants does a boy need?

We sauntered upstairs. After much deliberation, Emma finally bought a classic navy-blue polo jumper with the American flag on the front.

'It's $150 dollars though,' she said, thinking hard about it. 'That's a lot of money.'

Simon was persuasive.

'Do you like it? Are you going to wear it? You can afford it, so buy it, stop worrying about it, Emm,' he cajoled.

She made the purchase.

I saw a Tommy Hilfiger puffa that I fell in love with, it was a classic Hilfiger utilising the colours of the American flag. It was a snip at $300, but feeling a bit overextended after my underpant spree, I held back. Before the trip was over though I would be back with my plastic at the ready.

Melanie B bought two Hilfiger puffas, one for her and one for her boyfriend Richard, Melanie C bought one for herself and Victoria bought various Hilfiger items for her boyfriend Stuart.

Suitably spent up, we reconvened and headed back to our transport outside, after The Girls had posed for Julian on the sidewalk with their carrier bags.

Next stop was Antique Boutique, a huge and very trendy shop on Broadway that sells second-hand clothes and jewellery.

This is Geri's sort of shop. She bought a few outfits and a saucy pair of frilly black knickers that would feature in quite a few photo sessions later. Melanie B went into the basement in search of a sheepskin coat and some dungarees. Emma bought some baby-doll jewellery. It was not really Victoria's sort of shop, though she tried on a few coats and helped the other Girls with their search through the endless racks, offering suggestions and encouraging comments.

Melanie C wasn't happy.

'I'm bored,' she said to Peter. 'I find shopping really boring, I'd rather be doing something else.' However, we made plans for her to visit Nike Town before we left, because she wanted to buy some new trainers and to peruse their sportswear.

Now absolutely loaded down with shopping bags, we drove to a photo studio in down-town Manhattan where The Girls were to be photographed and interviewed for *Interview* magazine.

The photographers, two Finnish guys, were building a set with about five hundred packets of Domino sugar as a backdrop. It was a sugar and Spice type concept. While they prepared that and as The Girls began their hair and make-up, we ordered some Chinese food 'to go'.

Melanie C and B were in high spirits and put on a Backstreet Boyz CD. Melanie C did an amazing take-off of them, right down to dance moves, facial expressions, everything. The rest of The Girls love it and always fall around when she does it.

The food arrived. There was enough to feed a small army. Peter started taking The Girls into a side-room to do their interviews for *Top Of The Pops* magazine. Katie Puckrik arrived. She was conducting the interview for *Interview*.

The jet lag was starting to kick in with Emma and Geri, with Geri feeling particularly weary. She went to lie down on a sofa in the corner of the room and had a snooze.

I went off to a health food store across the road to buy an aloe vera drink for Melanie C. While there, I bought a tonic drink for Geri which had Ginkgo Bilboa and ginseng in it. I figured this would perk her up a bit. I also discovered a product called New York Stress Tablets, which contain camomile and valerian and help with, surprisingly enough, stress.

Back at the shoot there had been a disaster. The wall of sugar, which had taken two hours to erect, had fallen down. It was explained that we had to leave at six p.m. – The Girls had to leave to prepare to go to an important dinner with MTV.

The photographers started hurriedly rebuilding their wall.

Geri woke up looking the worse for wear and thanked me for the drink and the stress tablets, drinking half of it and leaving the rest she went to do her interview with Peter.

He was jubilant.

'I knew it. I just knew it,' he crowed.

Earlier he'd said 'I bet you Victoria has one of those lawn-mowers that you sit on and drive around your lawn, she's that Posh.' And surprise, surprise: he was absolutely right.

'She was brilliant,' he beamed, 'Victoria is so funny, she's got a brilliant sense of humour. I think she's given the best interview by far.'

Melanie B and Melanie C are peaking now. They've put some ruff drum 'n' bass on the stereo and both are freaking out and doing a mad dance routine in the middle of the studio. After this they will flop, the jet lag kicking in, and like everyone else they will start to be tired and a little grumpy.

The wall of sugar is finally held together with lashings of Sellotape and The Girls are shot against it individually, to be joined together magically by computer.

We beat a swift departure. We all head back to The Royalton for a drink before The Girls go off to woo MTV. There was a slight problem. During her interview with Peter, Geri saw written down in his notebook something about her nude modelling. It has put her on her guard. And, given her jet lagged and thoroughly exhausted state, she didn't have her normal re-sources to cope with it.

I took her off to one side and reassured her that Peter would never do anything to stitch her up.

'Look, this is for *Top Of The Pops*, not the *NME*,' I said consolingly. 'Peter would never do anything or write anything nasty about you.' My trust in Peter is implicit, he is one of my favourite editors and I consider him a true friend. Geri's paranoia was infectious, because even as I was giving her my reassurance, I caught myself at the same time thinking 'Peter's not out to stitch us up is he?' before immediately dismissing the idea, angry with myself that I could have even thought of it in the first place.

Concerned about Geri, I left a message on her voicemail that night while she was at the MTV dinner saying it was just a simple misunderstanding and if she wanted to talk about it, or just talk, then give me a call. She didn't ring.

Meanwhile, I'd spoken to Peter. He was horrified that Geri thought he had any kind of hidden agenda and he said he would talk to her about it the next day.

Tuesday dawned and we met The Girls at their hotel to drive off to the offices of *Teen Beat* magazine and *16* magazine, which are the two biggest teen magazines in America.

We waited in the lobby. One of the editors came out to greet us. She was clearly not happy. Firstly, she asked Joe Dyer to stop filming. No, she would not be happy to feature in *Spice – The Video*; no, it wasn't possible to go in to their offices, we would have to wait in the lobby and do the interview in the lobby.

Emma said, 'We've got up early to come down and talk to these people and they don't want us here and they're making us sit out in the lobby.'

There was a perceived sense that they thought we were all a bunch of freaks who might wreck their offices. This feeling was intensified when I was refused admission to their offices to use the toilet.

'Oh you can't go in there,' the receptionist said with distaste. 'It's just company regulations sir, no unauthorised personnel.'

The Girls were not happy.

I trotted down to the nearest deli, used the loo and bought

some mineral water and Diet Cola. On my return, two writers had joined this senior staff member and are half-heartedly and uninterestedly asking about the band's history and what they think of New York?

The Girls start taking the Mickey relentlessly, their humour floating way above the heads of the put-upon Teeners. The Girls have a wild anarchic streak, each egging the other on to see who can say the most outrageous thing to the interviewer but it's like a competition to put it over without being caught out. It's the spirit of the Sex Pistols all over again.

We left with the bad taste in our mouths redeemed by the notion that The Girls had got their own back by telling them a pack of lies.

We drove to the Flat Iron building to take some more photos and then arranged to meet back at the Royalton in the evening to take photos of The Girls in their suites.

The next day before they fly on to LA for further pre-promotion, they drove round to our hotel, Le Parker Meridian, so that we could perform our final shoot of them out on the roof, with Our Girls dwarfed by the phalanx of skyscrapers that dominated the skyline behind them.

The visit was deemed a success by all parties, particularly Virgin America who said they had never seen a group work harder or make such an impact with the radio programmers.

We would be back in two months' time, only this time The Spice Girls wouldn't be dominated by anyone or anything. They would be perched on top of the American charts, sitting oh so pretty, on top of the world.

And I'm totally not kidding, already.

Chapter Four

• •

WE'RE DREAMING OF
A SPICE CHRISTMAS

London, December 1996

As the year raced to its end, we were gearing up for our 'big Christmas push': we weren't only going to take Leningrad, but Moscow as well, with the Christmas double Number One slot our goal.

There was plenty to occupy our minds.

Imminent was the *Smash Hits* awards ceremony and show at the London Arena, where twelve thousand screaming fans would be waiting to see The Girls in the flesh. Later on that week The Spice Girls were going to be warming up a few Lapps when they took 170 children to the Arctic Circle to meet Father Christmas.

On top of these two excursions we also had seven magazine covers to shoot that week to tie in with the release of '2 Become 1' on 16 December, not to mention countless television appearances.

We gathered at London Docklands Arena at three p.m. on the Saturday to meet Nikki Chapman, The Girls' TV plugger, and while they had their hair and make-up attended to by Karin Darnell and Jenni Roberts, I spent my time mingling with the *Smash Hits* team who were all very busy making sure everything was running smoothly and went out of their way to make sure everyone was made to feel welcome and looked after. The rest of my time was spent answering my mobile phone, which never seemed to stop ringing these days.

There was a bit of tension backstage when ex-Take That singer Robbie Williams was thrown out of the dressing room he was supposed to be sharing with Mark Morrison. Morrison menacingly claimed the room for himself and his moody entourage.

The Girls were annoyed when they heard about it.

'What a prat!' said Melanie B.

'Return of The Prat!' quipped Geri.

All The Girls fell about laughing and started singing to the tune of 'Return of The Mack', Morrison's chart smash: 'Return of The Prat'.

After The Girls finished their hair and make-up and had performed the first run through, I brought a journalist backstage for a magazine interview which lasted about an hour.

We then left for the Britannia Hotel where The Girls were to be interviewed by Rowland Rivron for Virgin *Inflight* and after, by Louise Gannon for the *Daily Express*.

As we were leaving, Geri and Melanie B wanted to go and sign autographs for the hundreds of fans waiting outside the Arena. However, we were running very late and we didn't have any security with us. Geri and Mel B were not happy when they were told we didn't have time.

'Geri, please, get in the car. You can go and do it when we get back. The fans will still be here, and besides we don't have any security with us now, it won't be safe. Please wait till we get back. We're running so late,' I implored sweetly.

'Oh, but they've been waiting ages. I want to do it now.'

Camilla Howarth, one of The Girls' PAs, gently persuaded her into the waiting Jag. As we drove by the fans Geri pushed half her body through the window and yelled: 'I'm sorry, we want to come over and talk to you, but they won't let us.'

At this there were screams and the crowd surged forward. A crush barrier was knocked over and some fans were seen falling down.

'See Geri,' said Camilla, chidingly, 'that's what happens when there's no security. People get hurt.'

We arrived back at the Arena and ordered some meals and drinks for The Girls. The drinks arrived but the food did not until five minutes before we were due to leave. The Girls and I sat round a table and in between mouthfuls of food, finished off their interview with Gannon, who noticed how tired they all were.

'We're knackered,' Victoria told her through dainty fork-fuls of steamed vegetables. 'For eight months we've been flying here, there and everywhere. It's been relentless. I was at home the other day sitting on the sofa like a zombie and my mum looked at me and said: "You poor kid, you look dreadful." We've been working non-stop for months. Underneath all this make-up, I've got black rings around my eyes.'

'It never stops,' added Mel C. 'Recently, when we did the video for "2 Become 1", at the same time we were doing something for MTV and an interview and photo session for the *NME*. Victoria said: "I feel like screaming!" and I felt exactly the same.'

'Yeah, we get these schedules every day,' chipped in Mel B. 'On them is what we are doing every minute of the day, quite often from six a.m. to midnight. You can't look at more than one day at a time, otherwise you'd go mad.'

But alas, the mad schedule was calling us back to the Arena and we had to return for another run through and a photo session and interviews with *Smash Hits*, but before that we grabbed half a dozen security guards and The Girls went to meet the fans.

'I've come all the way from Cleethorpes to see you,' cried one.

'Geri, Geri, I love you, did you get my letter?' screamed a teenage boy.

'You are most definitely a Spice Boy,' she responded, giving him a big kiss, which left him with a wodge of lipstick on his face. His friends laughed at him.

'I'm never gonna wash that off, I love you, Geri!'

Geri looked very pleased.

'Victoria, over here!!!'

People shouted, trying to get all The Girls to look in their direction for photos.

'Melanie! Melanie!'

Melanie walked over and signed a photo for a girl in a baby-doll dress.

We cut it short as The Girls were due on stage, and headed back to the dressing room, which they were sharing with Gina G.

The next day, The Girls would pick up three awards for Best New Act, Best British Group and Best Video for 'Say You'll be There' and the show would be broadcast live on BBC 1 to thirty million people. We had extra security on stand-by, just in case we had to hustle The Girls through an even bigger mêlée of note-book-carrying NUJ members and paparazzi.

Round about eleven p.m., I got a call from a friend who had gone to King's Cross to collect the papers for me, and the *People* had run a story taken from an interview The Girls did with *Select*, with the headline 'I WANNA BE GAY SAYS SPICE GIRL

MEL'. In the original interview with Gina Morris, when asked if she would sleep with a woman, Melanie B replied: 'Yes, I would. I'm pretty liberated. It doesn't bother me. I think you are what you are.' Geri was quoted as saying: 'It's like asking "Would you ever eat strawberry ice cream?" If you've never tried it you don't know if you like it or not.'

The following morning after reading the *People* piece, Melanie B had everyone at the soundcheck in stitches when, while testing her microphone, she announced: 'Hello everybody, I'm gay today.'

We finished about one a.m. and had to be back at the Arena, next morning at eight a.m. for hair and make-up.

Backstage on the Sunday, it was a hive of activity, every few feet there was a pop star talking to another pop star. It was pop heaven. Ooh look, there's Louise, Ant & Dec, Peter André, East 17, Eternal, and Mark Morrison. They were all there.

While Morrison was on stage, Geri and Melanie B decided it would be a good idea to break into his dressing room and scrawl 'Return of The Prat!' on his mirror in pink lipstick. They were beside themselves with laughter afterwards. I voiced some concern.

'So what?' says Melanie B.

'Oh calm down, Muff,' chimed Geri, 'we're only having a laugh.'

'I know that, Geri,' I replied, 'but the man is up on a charge of armed robbery, and if he feels humiliated in front of the posse that he's got with him, then there's no telling what he, or one of his mates, might do.'

'Muff, chill out,' said Melanie B completely unconcerned. 'We can look after ourselves, mate. We're not worried about 'im.'

I gathered Nikki Chapman, Camilla Howarth and Emile

(Jerry Judge was away on another gig) from Music and Artists Security outside the dressing room for a pow-wow.

'We've got to be extra vigilant today because Geri and Melanie B have just been into Mark Morrison's dressing room and scrawled "Return of The Prat" in lipstick on his mirror,' I informed them. 'And I'm very worried about possible repercussions. All it would take is a smack in the mouth from him or one of his crew just before The Girls go onstage to ruin everything, let's not forget this is a live show.'

'I'll keep my eye on them,' said Nikki, with a now anxious expression on her face that matched my own. Emile promised not to let them out of his men's sight.

Although they sometimes gave me heart attacks, and extra cause for concern, at the same time I did love it when The Girls did something like this – it was their punky couldn't-care-less attitude and sense of fun that kept things interesting.

Despite the *Sun* declaring 'war', peace kept breaking out but in my role as the great appeaser, unlike Neville Chamberlain, I didn't have a piece of paper in my hand, no, I had something else: I had exclusive photos.

After the morning run through, we had an appointment with Andy Coulson who was coming along to have his picture taken with The Girls and one of the awards (for Best New Act) which had been sponsored by the *Sun*. The Girls had their hair and make-up touched up and then we went down to meet Coulson and his photographer Dave Hogan.

' 'Allo, Andy,' said Emma.

'All right, Girls?' he said chirpily.

'Hello, Andy,' said Geri.

'Hiya, Andy,' said Mel C.

Melanie B walked into the room with her face held with a forced false smile, extending her hand in a stiff handshake.

'Hello, Andy, you're my "friend" aren't you? My very good

SPICED UP!

friend.' She dropped the smile. 'Why do you say you're the friend of the stars when you're not? You're not my friend,' she said scornfully.

The week before, the *Sun* had printed an intrusive spread on Melanie and printed a topless picture of her on the beach, which a friend who lived in the same street as her mum had sold to them.

He looked uncomfortable and I tried to plaster things over with a bit of PR bluster.

'Errr, right, is everyone here? Is everyone ready? Dave, where do you want everyone then?'

The photo duties duly dispensed with in about two minutes, The Girls wandered back to their dressing room. Coulson and I were on eggshells, and tactfully avoided mentioning Melanie's comments.

I told him we were going to the Arctic Circle later that week and would like to offer him an 'exclusive' on the photos. I also told him that as well as that, I was setting up something special which would be 'exclusive' to the *Sun*. It would be something we'd give him for when The Girls got to Number One with '2 Become 1'.

I told Coulson it would be tailor-made especially for the *Sun* and that the editor and he were going to love it.

'Can't you tell us what it is?'

'Andy, I can't tell you now, it's a surprise, but you're going to love it, mate. Let's just say it's a Christmas present from The Girls to the *Sun*.'

'All right, we'll wait and see, Muff; and you will get the Lapland shots to Dominic in the office on Sunday, won't you?'

'I'll be in the office Sunday morning, mate, and I'll cab them over to Dominic . . .'

I'd been on the phone to my sister, Jody Dunleavy, who was head of press at EMI Records. She had been brilliant all the way through – only a phone call away. Someone I could call on whenever it got too much for me; she understood what I had to deal with every day and was a constant source of advice, support and encouragement. She is fab and I love her dearly.

I was on the phone to her and I was in a bit of a predicament. As part of our push for Christmas chart domination, and because we hadn't really done much with them so far, we planned to do something with the *Mirror*. They'd offered us five straight days of features in the week of the release of '2 Become 1', which was perfect. We were to do a shoot with their fashion editor and a different Girl would feature each day as part of their 'World's Most Beautiful Women' series.

The thing was, I needed some insurance to keep the *Sun* happy while this was going on, to keep them off our backs.

'What can I do?' I asked my sister.

'What can you offer the *Sun* as "exclusives"?' Jody asked.

'Well, I'm already giving them the Lapland shots as an exclusive when we come back next week. I need something I can hold over till we go to Number One.'

'Can you do something else in Lapland and hold it back for them?'

'Mmm, maybe something with Father Christmas, 'cause they'll be Number One at the start of Christmas week so that would be topical.'

'How about you get some dummy copies of the *Sun* made up with a seasonal greeting from The Girls?' she said.

'Jodes, you are a genius and I love you! Thank you very much. That's brilliant!'

'You could get The Girls holding up copies of the *Sun* that read "Merry Christmas from The Spice Girls" or something.'

Fantastic. So when the *Sun* phoned up and started whinging when the *Mirror* pieces started to run, we could say, 'Yeah, OK, but just wait until you see what we've got for you for next Monday!'

So that was what we planned to do.

The rest of the day passed quickly, in a blur of hair and make-up and The Girls hanging out mainly with East 17, whom they get on really well with.

I was standing in the corridor outside the dressing room with Victoria who was talking to Tony Mortimer. Karin, our lovely make-up woman, came out and wanted to apply some cream to Victoria's legs, to stop them shining on television. Apparently this is a routine process. She started to apply the cream to Victoria's legs, rubbing it in vigorously.

Tony Mortimer said: 'Are you going to do me next?'

'Yeah, if you like,' replied Karin.

'Oh nice one,' said Tony, and without another word he undid his trousers, which dropped like a stone, and stood there calmly while Victoria collapsed in fits of giggles.

The tension grew as showtime approached. The bands milled around the long corridor backstage, chatting, laughing and warming up. Then it was time. Five security guards escorted The Girls to the side of the stage.

The Girls pulled off an amazing routine and everyone was in agreement that they'd stolen the show. Once again they were buzzing. The crowd went mental. This was the first time they'd performed to an audience this size and they'd loved every minute of it. As soon as they came off stage after lining up with everyone for the finale they were herded straight to the stage door where the Jags were lined up, engines running with The Girls' bags already packed and in the boot.

'Go, Go, Go!' They were hustled out of the door, past the

waiting cameramen and into the cars. It was business as usual at the end of a very busy day.

But, if that was a busy day, just take a look at the schedule for the next few days: up at six a.m., The Girls were driven to a community centre in Birmingham, which had been converted into a photo studio for the day to shoot a cover for *Sky* magazine. From there they were to perform a PA as part of the opening celebrations of Tower Records in Birmingham and to recieve a disc for the millionth copy of 'Wannabe' sold in the UK.

The day after that was another nightmare, with three photo sessions, for *90 Minutes*, the *Big Issue* and *Vanity Fair*. A rare day off in between and then the day after Lapland was followed by the National Lottery show. What a week!

I met the hair and make-up people at Euston Station in the morning and we arrived at the Ladywood Arts and Leisure Centre at around nine a.m. The Girls arrived dead tired at ten thirty. They were knackered. They started to get their hair and make-up done and the morning settled into a relaxed sort of pace, punctuated by me handing each of The Girls my mobile phone from time to time. They give good phone calls, passing comment on topics from *Star Wars* to the chances of Liverpool doing the double. The Spice Girls' opinions are sought by newspapers and magazines on absolutely anything and everything . . .

Damon Syson, interviewing for *Sky*, took The Girls off to one of the changing rooms to talk.

Emma and Melanie C were bored. Out of all of The Girls, they like doing interviews the least. I once asked them what they thought of a newspaper feature that had taken a lot of time and certainly a lot of trouble, not to mention a few fair quid, to arrange and implement.

'Me and Emm, we started reading it on the plane the other day,' Melanie C informed me, 'but we gave up halfway through, 'cause it was dead boring,' giving me one of her disarming, sweet smiles that make you forgive anything.

Today's interview was 'boring'. They reluctantly talked to the guy and were relieved when we ran out of time and had to head off to Tower Records. I asked if it was OK for him to share their car on the way back.

'Oh yeah, no problem,' they said, but were horrified when they discovered I meant in the car on the way back to London, not down the road to Tower Records.

'Oh Muff, please, we're really knackered,' said Emma sweetly. 'We don't mind him coming in the car on the way to the shop, but not back to London, we want to rest.' He travelled in the car on the way to Tower, where we lost him in the crush.

Thousands and thousands of people had packed the streets around the shop. We drove round to the back entrance which backed on to a building site. About thirty builders were hanging over the scaffolding, doing what builders do best: wolf-whistling the arrival of our gorgeous charges.

One of the pot-bellied gents roared in a thick brummy accent: 'Geri, I love you.'

She yelled back: 'I love you too! Come on you Spice Boys!'

Everyone roared with laughter.

Inside, the shop was as chaotic as outside.

The Girls answered a set of questions asked by BRMB DJ Paul Hollins in a casual question/answer way. Reef had been playing a little earlier and Melanie B took over their drum kit, giving her best Keith Moon impersonation. Someone threw a huge pair of underpants up on the stage and Geri examined them closely for skid-marks. Then they held a draw to see which lucky person was going to win a platinum disc and sixteen-year-old

Paul Mullen went home to Great Barr, a very happy Spice Boy indeed.

After The Girls finished and just before we left, we brought them back into a sealed off area to have their picture taken with a disc commemorating a million sales. A few freelance photographers had managed to get into the room and, despite my insistence that this was a private area and my request that they stop shooting, their motor-drives kept turning over.

'Security!' I yelled in a high-pitched voice, to try and get them removed. Victoria and Catri Drummond (one of The Girls' PA's and Simon Fuller's girlfriend) found this hilarious and took the mickey out of me for days afterwards, screaming 'Security' in their best falsetto whenever they saw me.

After this, Jerry Judge led us through the throng of photographers, reporters and fans to a point near the entrance where he gave us a quick briefing. We were all to leave in one limo, with about nine of us piling in and then meeting the usual Jags and drivers at a garage about five miles down the road.

'Listen,' said Jerry, 'there's about ten thousand people gathered outside that front door. Now, when you leave, I don't want any of you to stop to sign autographs because it isn't safe. The barriers will just topple over if you do that. It's a mad scrum out there and people will just get hurt. Does everyone understand?'

Everyone nodded their understanding.

'Just walk through that door and get straight into the car, you can wave, but don't stop for anything. OK, Girls?'

'OK, Jerry,' replied The Girls together. Adding in chorus: 'Thanks, Jerry.'

'OK, here we go,' he said leading us down the stairs to the door.

Once through the door, we were deafened by the screams and almost blinded by the flash of a thousand cameras going off.

We piled into the car, falling on top of one another, and when we were all in, Jerry closed the door after us and told the driver to step on it.

What seemed like a thousand hands pummelled on every part of the Daimler. The windows were obscured by palms, the bodywork rang with the sound of mad thumpings, interspersed with hysterical screams.

We picked ourselves up off the floor and breathlessly re-arranged ourselves on the seats.

'Blimey!' declared Melanie B, stunned.

'This is really crazy,' said Geri, huskily. 'Now I know how The Beatles must have felt.'

'Oh I wish my mum was here to see this,' said Emma.

'My mum is going to be really pleased that we got a bigger crowd than Fergie,' said Victoria, with an extremely pleased look on her face. The Duchess of York had been signing books just up the road a couple of hours earlier and told reporters: 'I like The Spice Girls, they're great for pop music especially because they're Girls. I have their CD in the car and sing along to it with Beatrice and Eugenie.'

At a service station about ten minutes later we separated into the usual convoy of Jaguars. I shared a Jag with Victoria and Catri and we headed straight back to London.

The next day, we assembled at Holborn Studios, strangely enough not in Holborn but in Islington, which we used often and where the covers were shot for *90 Minutes*, a football magazine, with The Girls in football strips, and the *Big Issue* for their Christmas edition. Straight after that we drove to the Eve Club on Regent Street where there was a shoot for the American magazine *Vanity Fair*. We were supposed to finish with a shoot of The Girls hanging from Eros at Piccadilly Circus at nine p.m. Just an average day in Spiceworld.

The Girls got dressed up in the football kits that they

requested. Being a Watford Girl, Geri had naturally chosen Watford, Melanie B donned a Leeds kit, Melanie C opted for Liverpool, of course, Emma picked Tottenham and Victoria – with a spookily prophetic choice – decided to go for Manchester United, for the reason that Simon Fuller supported them. Her aesthetic sensibilities were offended by the strip though.

'Oh, I wish I'd chosen Tottenham or Chelsea now,' she moaned. 'It's just horrible, that colour, it's really not me at all, I only chose it because Simon supports them. I don't want to have Sharp plastered all over my chest.'

'Well, it could be worse, look, I've got "CTX Computer Products" over mine, Vic,' said Geri, squeezing into the tiniest pair of football boots you ever did see.

I wonder if Victoria still feels that way about the Man United strip, or whether for some reason or other she now holds a different opinion.

At the end of the interview she was shown photographs of footballers and asked to name them. 'Ooh, he's nice. Who's that?' she asked excitedly. 'David Beckham. He plays for Manchester United,' the interviewer replied.

'Oh, I'll go up there then, we can go out for dinner afterwards.'

The Girls looked fabulous in their kit, and for photographer Derek Ridgers, they struck a penalty wall pose with their hands over their nether regions, looking both extremely saucy and very, very funny. They all enjoyed it as it was something a little bit different to the thousands of sessions they now had under their belts.

After changing and a break for a late lunch we motored through the *Big Issue* sesh with Rankin taking the photos and Sheryl Garratt, former editor of *The Face*, performing the interview honours. Was it really seven o'clock already?

Seita Neiland, The Girls' stylist reappeared with Danielle, her assistant and a whole shop full of clothes which The Girls picked through as though tearing apart a Bargain Bin. Michael Roberts, the photographer for *Vanity Fair*, had requested warm and vibrant colours for his session and The Girls got dressed accordingly.

We drove to the Eve Club, where Christine Keeler had hung out in the 1960s and which was mentioned in the Profumo Scandal, to meet Emma Forrest who was writing the piece. The Girls were then introduced to Michael.

We had brought security with us for the Eros shot, which a little later Michael cancelled, deciding he'd already got what he wanted. We asked security to clear out some reps from Grolsch, whom the owner of the Eve had taken upon himself to invite to our session for an ogle.

'Sorry, but we're not goldfish, all right,' said Melanie B, out loud to no one and everyone in particular.

'Yeah, we're not animals in a zoo,' added Emma.

The Girls hate being watched while they're working.

By nine thirty p.m. we'd finished and just before The Girls left I asked them to sign a copy of the *NME* cover that I was going to get framed. One copy (signed, for me) and a copy for each of The Girls and Simon Fuller.

We next met at Gatwick Airport to board a specially chartered plane that was taking 150 competition winners plus Melanie B's and C's nieces and nephews, photographer Ray Burmiston, Robert Sandall and assorted MTV camerawomen and European press types to Rovaniemi, home to Santa Claus Village on the Arctic Circle

After we had boarded the plane, The Girls filled up the first class section, but when we had taken off, they wasted no time in coming down and saying 'Hi!' to everyone, posing for photos, with Geri taking it upon herself to play hostess with the mostest, pouring out tea and coffee, while Emma spoonfed some of the babies on board.

I gave each of The Girls a copy of that morning's *Daily Star*. We had given them some Ellen Von Unwerth shots as an 'exclusive' and not only had we made the front page, but they had turned one of the shots into a double-page poster.

Some of Melanie C's nephews were excitable about the trip, to say the least, and were running up and down the plane going completely bonkers. Now, what was it W C Fields said about never working with children or reindeers? I took it upon myself to become Mr Grumpy and (with the kids at least) Mr Unpopular, bellowing at them that: 'THIS IS NOT A PLAYGROUND! THIS IS AN AEROPLANE! NOW GET BACK TO YOUR SEATS AND STAY THERE!'

Rather bizarrely, they complied. A few of the grown-ups proffered thumbs up signs. Now, hopefully, we could relax for the six and a half hour flight.

The children eyed me very suspiciously. They were certain that I was a madman and to be avoided at all costs.

On arrival at Rovaniemi, Santa Claus and his elves plus a couple of reindeers were there to greet us. I arranged for Ray Burmiston to get off the plane first, so he was ready to take a picture of The Girls leaving the plane together. I tried to arrange it that The Girls all left in a group with the PAs and so on walking behind, but this didn't happen and the shot was messed up. I always think of classic Beatles' shots on occasions like this and how they were set up.

Later, I made a point of telling the PAs Camilla and Rachel that in future, when The Girls leave a plane and there may be photographers present, always to make sure they leave first and together. Think photo. Think history. That's what one should always do in PR terms: maintain a sense of the historic.

We loaded all our luggage into one of the coaches and were then driven the short drive to Santa Claus Village. Once there, The Girls were ensconced around Santa in his Grotto and the competition winners took it in turns to have their photos taken with The Girls and Santa, while Sybil Ruskill and Di Carter, the lovely camerawomen from MTV, filmed the entire event.

While this was going on, I pulled The Girls' luggage off their bus and carried it through the ice and snow to the dressing room, which Santa had kindly vacated so they could change for the *Sun* 'exclusive', which we were going to shoot as soon as all the competition winners had finished. We didn't have much time – about twenty minutes in all – because, as usual, we were on a busy schedule and had borrowed this time from the international department at Virgin who had set the trip up. Lorraine Barry, the lovely and sparky head of the international department, and Bart Cools, international manager, were always moaning that I stole their time on trips like this. So, I endeavoured not to keep The Girls for too long.

We had a last-minute disaster. Emma's case had gone back to the hotel on the other bus. All The Girls had brought a red outfit for the seasonal photograph.

'Look, is there something you could borrow from one of the other Girls for the photo, Emm?'

'No, I need my bag, I brought a costume especially.'

'How about if you borrowed something red from Santa? It's just we don't have much time.'

'No, Muff, I really need what's in my bag.'

'OK, no problem, Emm, I'll see if we can get a taxi to pick it up from the hotel.'

Which is what we did. While we waited for it to return, I helped Ray Burmiston to set up his lights for the shoot, gave

Rachel Pinfold, who had the unenviable job of looking after all the nieces and nephews, some money for burgers and Coke, and made sure The Girls were getting along OK.

I had brought along five 'Santa' hats.

'Muff, if you think I'm wearing one of those hats, you've got another thing coming,' said Melanie B, forcefully.

'Unless one of them is made by Gucci, or Prada, then I'm with Melanie on that one,' added Victoria, with a grin.

'Geri?' I looked over quizzically.

'Forget it, Muff.'

'Melanie,' looking at Sporty.

'Leave it out, will ya,' she said, laughing.

I didn't even bother to ask Emma. Instead, I went outside to see if Baby's outfit had arrived and had a minor heart attack when I saw that in the permanent camera booth opposite Santa, they had fed the image of The Girls on to the Internet. I politely had a freak out.

'Oh, no, no, no, no, no, no. I'm sorry. This is not good. We can't have images of The Girls going out on the Internet. We're very grateful for you letting us be here, but I'm sorry this is not good.'

I had visions of my 'exclusive' landing on a billion Web sites around the world – two weeks *before* I'd given it to the *Sun*. The man in the booth switched off the images and promised not to film what was about to follow.

Emma's costume turned up and she got dressed. The Girls looked fabulous when they finally came out of the dressing room. They arranged themselves around Santa, then we positioned the elves. I distributed the dummy copies of the *Sun* among Santa and the elves and then Ray Burmiston took over.

'Looking lovely, Girls. Nice smiles please. Thank you. Three, two, one.' Flash! 'Thank You, Girls. Again. Three, two, one.' Flash! 'Thank you, ladies. Geri, move in a bit, Victoria, if you could move to the left a touch, Melanie C stay where you are. That's great, Emma and Melanie B come forward a bit. Thank you. Now Santa, can you give us a bit more beard please . . . ?'

I thought it would be better if Santa and the elves held the papers, because the message still came across and The Girls could concentrate on looking gorgeous.

'Girls, we want this to be one of those shoo-be-doo-be-doo moments, all calm and heavenly. Think heaven and angels and that sort of thing,' Ray said inspiringly.

'Just pretend you're all virgins again,' I shouted.

'You don't know just how true that is,' answered Melanie C.

When Ray announced it was a wrap, I passed him my camera and went to sit on the floor in front of Santa, The Girls sitting demurely all around me.

'Touch the head of the Buddha,' shouted Geri, as she and Emma placed their hands on my shaven head, Melanie C linked her arm through mine and Melanie B gave me a little squeeze. I felt very emotional and pleased that I'd captured a magic Spiceworld moment for posterity.

As Ray and I broke the equipment down, The Girls changed and went with Simon Fuller to the canteen for a drink and a snack. We then headed back to the Hotel Vakuna where we showered and then went to choose our thermal wear. We were going to eat dinner in a giant igloo where even the tables and chairs were made of ice, so this attire was essential.

The Girls loved the clobber. We all wore red and blue suits, The Girls having distinctive yellow and purple combinations so that they stood out from the crowd, although Emma found she was too small for the yellow and purple and with some reluctance slid into a red and blue suit. Geri thought the suits were great.

'The brilliant thing about these suits,' she said, 'is that they hide a multitude of sins. If you're having a fat day, these are the best.'

'These boiler-suit things that we have to wear,' explained Scary, 'they're like a uniform, but I refuse to conform completely because I'm wearing me own boots!'

We were driven by coach to the Ice Queen's Igloo. On arrival, there was a reindeer ride by sleigh across a field to the igloo. It was freezing inside, literally. But as the evening wore on, our body heat and breath started to make the ice tables melt and everything became very slushy.

The Girls arrived later than the rest of us because they had been doing their MTV interview with Sybil and Di. I spent the rest of the evening running round organising what Ray and I call 'Kodak moments' – groovy shots or set-ups, with baby reindeer, snowball fights and so on.

By the time we got back to the hotel it was one a.m., my cream was crackered and I was fit only for sleep, but I was persuaded to visit briefly the Hotel Club – the snappily titled 'Doris Disco' – where a mutitude of very drunk Finns staggered awkwardly across the floor to ABBA and A-HA ditties. I guess that is what's meant by Lapp dancing.

Melanie B soon showed them how it should be done and somehow she and Geri stayed up till four a.m., leading the party posse on a spree that only stopped when the bar ran out of alcohol.

Poor Rachel had her work cut out as the hyper-active nephews did not go to sleep until five a.m. (and that was only after they had drained the contents of their mini-bar!) and ran her ragged around the hotel corridors for endless hours.

At nine the next morning, we went on a visit to a reindeer farm which is inside the Arctic Circle. We were all given a certificate to commemorate our presence there and then embarked on another reindeer ride, The Girls taking part in a ritual which involved daubing their faces with charcoal which ensures they will come back as reindeer in their next lives.

'As long as I'm not going to be eaten,' Victoria told us.

'I want to come back as Rudolph,' said Geri, 'then I could drink as much as I like, and because I've got a red nose no one would be any the wiser, would they?'

It was then time for us to embark on a snowmobile ride. Melanie B drove with Melanie C on the back. Geri took Victoria and Emma was driven by Simon. I got on the back with Robert Sandall at the helm.

A word of advice. Never, ever, go on the back of a snow-mobile. Always insist on driving. On the back it's like being on a bucking bronco, especially if the terrain is bad. I was thrown all over the place and when we got back to England that night I discovered I had a horrendous back injury, which took three weeks and a king's ransom spent on chiropractors, shiatsu, osteopaths and physiotherapy to heal.

Being thrown all over the place at ninety miles an hour gives you quite an appetite and on our return lunch was ready.

Our repast? Reindeer and mash. Hmm, yummy.

All morning The Girls acted like they were big kids, leading the little kids in snowball fights and slalom races down the icy slopes. All too soon it was time to get on the coach with our wet arses and head for the airport. Not before I'd taken the opportunity, though, to phone a few people on my mobile to let them know I was phoning from the Arctic Circle. What a poseur.

Once on the plane, as The Girls had been giving their all for at least the last twenty-six hours, they flopped into their seats and fell asleep. But they were disturbed by the nephews and nieces who kept walking through and waking them.

'It's not fair,' said a tired and grumpy Melanie B. 'We're knackered. Please, we'll talk to yer before we reach London, but we need a little sleep now. All right? Thank you.'

I gave the kids my rejected Santa hats as consolation. *They* seem quite pleased with them.

After we landed at Gatwick and before The Girls were whisked away in their Jaguars, they said ta-ta.

'Thanks for coming every-bod-e-e-e-e-e-e!' yelled Scary.

'It was really good to see you all,' screeched Geri. 'It wouldn't have been half as much fun without you. Girl Power!'

On Saturday, I spent a rare day off in the Accident and Emergency department having my back X-rayed, which isn't ideal, followed by a Sunday morning in the office approving the Lapland shots and getting them over to the *Sun*. The Girls had also had no respite. Yesterday was the Lottery show, today was the Children's ITV awards.

I had just got back and was lying on the living-room floor in agony when the EastEnders omnibus was interrupted by my mobile phone ringing. I have to have it switched on twenty-four hours a day. Just in case.

'Ahh Muff, Lee Harpin here.' Lee is a writer for the *Daily Star*.

'Hello mate. What's up?'

'Well, you know you're coming in tomorrow. Which we're all looking forward to, it's just that we've had this human interest story come in about this boy with cerebral palsy, Daniel Williams, whose mum claims that he couldn't walk until he heard 'Wannabe'. Apparently, now every time he hears it, he gets up and does a little dance.'

'Oh bloody hell, Lee,' I groaned, 'so The Girls are performing miracles now are they?'

'Well, it would appear so, yes,' he said with a chuckle.

'Oh leave it out, mate,' I giggled.

'Not only are they as popular as Jesus, they would seem to be equally as efficacious,' he said drily. 'Talk about Girl Power!'

'Lee, where did this story originate?'

He gave me the name of a Northern news agency that had

been trying to run dodgy stories on Our Girls for months.

'Aah! Well, that explains it, mate.'

'So can you give me a quote then?'

'I'll have to call you back, mate.'

I left a message on Simon's and Gerrard Tyrell's machines. Gerrard called back. We decided on an innocuous quote, saying The Girls were very happy that little Daniel Williams had made a wonderful recovery.

Next morning, I stopped at a newsagents on my way to The Savoy, where we had booked a suite for The Girls to attend to their hair and make-up before we went to the *Daily Star* for the phone-in.

'SPICE GIRLS MADE MY BOY WALK!' was the front-page headline.

We had arranged with Linda Duff, pop correspondent at the *Daily Star*, to go into the newspaper's office to talk to the fans on five phonelines for an hour. Take That had done something similar a couple of years earlier to scenes of complete mayhem outside, with police and security holding back thousands of screaming, tearful fans. The newspaper has been trailing the event for the last week, though it had refrained from announcing the time and day The Girls would be at the offices, until today's paper, which stated we would be there and on the phones from twelve thirty to one thirty p.m.

I had booked ten extra security guards to be on the safe side.

While at the Savoy, my mobile phone rang. It was Linda Duff.

'Aah, hello, Muff,' her rich Southern Irish accent filled my left ear.

'Hello, Linda, how're we getting on, are you ready for us down there?'

'Oh yes, the champagne is on ice, the phones are already ringing and your security guys are down here liaising with our security guys and the police.'

'Are there many fans there, yet?' I asked.

'Well, not that many yet,' she said, 'it is a school day, but hopefully by the time you arrive . . . Listen, Muff, I want to ask you something . . .'

'Y-e-s,' I replied slowly.

'Well, you know the little boy in the paper today, we've brought him and his mum down to London to meet The Girls. Is that OK?'

It was far from OK. It seemed every time we did something with one of the tabloids, they deviated from the agreed agenda and ended up trying to do a number on us. Linda knew that if she'd asked in advance we would have said *no*. It's not that The Girls are lacking in compassion in any way, it was just they were being used.

'I'm not happy about this, Linda,' I told her, 'and I know Simon Fuller won't be happy either. You know this puts the phone-in in jeopardy don't you?'

She knew I was bluffing – we had all gone too far to blow out the phone-in – but she played along.

'Aah, Muff, I'm really sorry, it's the editors here, they've gone and done it behind my back. And the little boy's here now so what can I do about it? I'm really sorry. They've got me over a barrel.'

To be more precise, they had got us over a barrel.

'Look, I'll have to call you back.'

I called Simon and although he was not happy either, we both agreed the best course of action was to plough on, let The Girls meet Daniel, let the *Star* take their pictures, do the phone-in and get the hell out of there.

I briefed The Girls on the new development and at midday

our cars left The Savoy and headed for Ludgate House, by Blackfriar's Bridge.

We were disappointed on reaching their office to see that our security guards outnumbered the fans. We counted three.

'And they were the girls who come into the office to sort out the fan mail,' said Melanie B, dejectedly.

We were greeted by Emile from Music and Artists Security, Linda and her husband, photographer Nick Tannesley and writer Rav Singh, who escorted us up to the office.

Once there, after the *Star*'s photographers had signed their release forms, The Girls met Mrs Williams and Daniel and posed with him for the cameras. Then, we were taken into the news editor's office where the phones were waiting. The next day, the *Star* would say they received seventy thousand calls in one hour. Despite the lack of fans outside, The Girls were deluged by calls, their admirers making up for what they lacked in travel skills, given the newspaper's failure to give The Girls' appearance advance notice with digit power.

Before we went in, I briefed The Girls to be careful on the phone as the calls would probably be recorded (they weren't) and to watch out as we might get journalists from other papers ringing up with tricky or subversive questions.

'Listen, my darlings,' I'd said at The Savoy. 'If anyone calls who sounds dodgy or who you don't like the sound of just put the phone down, OK?'

An old friend of Melanie B called whom she hadn't seen for years. They had a good chat and Melanie took her number and promised to stay in touch.

Geri got the obligatory perv phoning in, who wanted to know what colour knickers she was wearing.

'Don't you read the papers? I never wear any, mate!' she said, before replacing the receiver and raising her eyes towards the heavens.

We kept being interrupted by *Star* staff, bursting in with armfuls of the poster they had printed the week before and demanding autographs. Emile was asked not to let anyone else disturb us.

After posing for some wacky photos for Nick Tannesley, we made our departure and headed off first to keep an appointment with *The Chart Show* and then to a photo session with *Top Of The Pops* magazine, where The Girls not only had a meeting with *Top Of The Pops* producer Rick Blaxhill, to discuss their presenting the Christmas edition of the show, but also with Simon Fuller's brother Kim to discuss his script for their forthcoming movie.

The next morning, the *Star*'s front page screamed: 'SPICE GIRLS INVADE STAR HQ!' However, we were far from happy because they had chosen to illustrate the piece with one of Geri's old glamour shots. The Girls and I were very upset about it. They had taken lots of new pictures the day before, and after we had gone in and met Daniel, this was how they repaid us.

I called Linda Duff.

'Linda, Muff.'

'Aah morning, Muff. Well, what d'ya think?'

'Linda, we are so upset I can't tell you.'

'You're joking,' she said, genuinely surprised. 'You've got the front page and seven pages inside and you're telling me you're upset?'

'Linda, why did you use that old picture of Geri on the front page?'

'Aah, now, that wasn't anything to do with me, that was the picture editor and the news editor.'

'Linda, how do you think Geri's feeling this morning? After we went out of our way to come down there and sort you lot out, you repay us by printing that picture of Geri. It's not as if Nick didn't get loads of new shots of the band yesterday, is it? The Girls are extremely disappointed and wonder why they bothered.'

'Aah well, I'm sorry they feel that way, Muff, but please don't take it out on me. We loved having you down here and meeting The Girls, and I'm sorry if this has spoiled it, but I think you've got a great spread and if you want to complain about it then please take your complaints to the picture editor and the news editor because they made the decision to hold the story up with a strong picture, not me. OK?'

We left it there. Both sides feeling aggrieved.

The next day we found out that the *People* was definitely going to run some pictures of Melanie C taken at a party the following Sunday. They would show other people (but not Melanie) allegedly taking cocaine. In the light of this, and given the fact that the *People* is a Mirror Group newspaper and we were supposed to be fulfilling our fashion session commitment with the *Mirror* that Saturday (to run all the following week), we decided that, in the circumstances, it would be best to blow the *Mirror* out.

We could not afford to take the risk that they would use the photos from the fashion stories to illustrate any potential follow-ups from the *People* story. As this was the second time things hadn't gone as smoothly as we hoped with the *Mirror*, I was beginning to feel that I definitely wouldn't be on their Christmas card list. I agonised over what reason I was going to give the fashion editor for blowing them out – after all, I wanted to play down the *People* thing as much as possible.

But just as I was about to bite the bullet, I got a call from Nikki Chapman who, unaware of the current circumstances, informed me that I was going to have to cancel the shoot with the *Mirror* on Saturday as The Girls were now going to appear on *Noel's House Party*. Thank you. There is a God after all!

By the time the *People* story came out on the Sunday, it was virtually ignored, completely overshadowed by another event created by The Spice Girls that had prompted a frenzied media avalanche.

Now, what is the biggest taboo for any aspirant pop group? What is the golden rule that has been carved in stone since time immemorial? The one thing that is considered commercial suicide? In the golden rule book of pop, this is the topic that dare not be mentioned by name. The one that you must never, ever, voice your opinions on in public?

Aah, yes. *Politics*.

Chapter Five

· ·

VOTE SPICE!

London, 13th December, 1996

'What I really want for Christmas is a Spice Girls LP.'

John Major

'John Major is a boring pillock.'

Posh Spice

So, by now we knew certain things about The Spice Girls. They were more important than Jesus. And they could perform miracles. But not even they could save the Tory Party. Not that that was ever their intention, though for a short time they were looked upon as the last hope by every Conservative newspaper proprietor and ham-strung Tory spin-doctor down at Central Office.

Friday, 13 December 1996 was a red-letter day. In more ways than one. It definitely wasn't a blue-letter day. It was the day the Tories got routed at the Barnsley by-election and the day I got up at six a.m. to go to my newsagents to find The Girls on the front page of every newspaper in the country.

When we decided to give an interview to the *Spectator*

magazine, we knew it would create some controversy, but the swift and overwhelming media response was more than we could ever have dreamed of. That Friday the thirteenth may have been unlucky for the Conservative government, in sounding their final death-knell, but it was the day that Posh, Sporty, Ginger, Scary and Baby went from being just plain everyday famous to becoming household names. It was the day that they crossed over from being pop stars to acquiring full-fledged celebrity status.

Victoria once said in an interview with *The Face*: 'We want to be household names like Fairy Liquid or Vim.' This was the day her wish came true.

The switchboard was jammed. Every line in the press office at Virgin was red-hot. People wanted The Girls' opinions on everything from Maastricht to mascara. The Girls were featured on BBC's Six O'clock News and ITV's *News at Ten*. Jeremy Paxman pondered the 'Spice Vote' on *Newsnight*. The Prime Minister talked about them on the *Today* programme on Radio 4. This was the day that every member of parliament and judge in the country finally knew what a 'Spice Girl' was.

The next day, we sold untold copies of their album *Spice*. Orders soared for their Christmas single '2 Become 1', which was to be released on Monday, 16 December.

Now, there was no escape from Girl Power!

When we had received the original request from writer Simon Sebag-Montefiore in mid-November, we were intrigued. The *Spectator* had offered us their Christmas Interview, which is normally reserved for the prime minister or political figures of similar stature.

The request had been considered carefully and discussed by Simon Fuller, Ray Cooper and myself. What The Girls lacked in gravitas, they certainly made up for with their candid opinions. We knew, as ever, that they were capable of looking after themselves. We were more worried for the welfare of Sebag-Montefiore.

The Christmas double issue of the *Spectator* was due to be published on 12 December, the day of the Barnsley by-election, and four days before the release of '2 Become 1'. The timing was perfect.

Best case scenario was that the humorous and outspoken nature of the article would be picked up by the national press and give us a splurge of publicity just as the new single came out, while the worst case scenario was that it would be totally ignored and do us no harm anyway. As part of our intention to constantly broaden the demographic and to always come up with the unexpected, we decided to steam ahead.

Simon Sebag-Montefiore met me at the rehearsals for the *Smash Hits* awards ceremony on Saturday, 30 November. After watching The Girls run through 'Wannabe' and 'Say You'll Be There' and after introducing him to Emma Cochrane, the associate editor of *Smash Hits*, I went to the dressing room and arranged five chairs in a semicircle facing Sebag-Montefiore's single seat.

I'd briefed The Girls beforehand, explaining what sort of a magazine the *Spectator* was and asked them just to relax, be themselves and have a bit of fun with it.

'Oh we will, Muff, don't worry,' said Geri, with an evil grin on her face.

'Oh, good,' said Victoria smiling, on hearing of the magazine's political leanings. 'My mum will be pleased.'

'My mum won't,' said Melanie C. 'We hate the Tories.'

'Just go and get him, Muff and let's get on with it,' said Melanie B impatiently.

After the introductions, Sebag-Montefiore got down to the nitty-gritty and asked The Girls their political affiliations.

'I'm an anarchist,' said Melanie B.

'My family votes Conservative,' said Victoria, 'I'd never vote Labour.' Which in the article mysteriously became the Royal 'we', as in 'We'd never vote Labour.'

'I'm from Liverpool and I vote Labour,' said Melanie C, earnestly.

'I'm not really political,' said Emma.

'I really admire Margaret Thatcher,' said Geri, 'she was the first Spice Girl, but I think a coalition would be best. I'm Conservative but I'm also a little bit Lib-Dem with a touch of Greenpeace.'

After a few minutes, he focused his attentions on Geri and Victoria who were saying the things he wanted to hear.

'How about a figure from history, whom you really admire?' he asked.

'Apart from Margaret Thatcher, Joan of Arc, she was an early advocate of Girl Power!' said Geri.

'Definitely Princess Diana, I'm a big fan of Princess Di's, I think she's wonderful,' said Victoria.

'Nelson Mandela,' said Melanie B.

'He doesn't count,' answered Sebag-Montefiore.

'Why not?' replied Melanie, irritated, 'I think he's an amazing man who has come through extreme suffering to bring about the emancipation of the South African people.'

'He's too contemporary,' Sebag-Montefiore replied brusquely, continuing with a sardonic look on his face. 'How about Pitt The Younger?'

'Who?'

'Who?'

'Who?'

'Who?'

'Who?'

After the interview was finished Melanie C came over to me.

'I didn't really enjoy that, Muff, he wasn't really listening to what Mel and I had to say, was he?'

'Well, no, not really. It didn't seem like it.'

'I hope this piece is going to be all right?'

'Melanie, if this piece works out the way we hope it does, we're going to get a lot of publicity out of it.'

'Well, I just hope you're right.'

The timing of the piece was also perfect in that the Tory press used the article to gloss over the fact that they'd just received a drubbing in the by-election and used the so-called 'views' of The Girls to try to bolster up a sagging regime. It was hilarious.

We lit the blue touch-paper and sat back and watched the resultant fireworks, cor-ing, aah-ing and laughing at each subsequent development and media conquest.

Deep analysis of their 'Thatcherite' lyrics followed in papers such as the *Daily Express*, Leader editorials in the broadsheets made pronouncements on the 'Spice Vote', questions were asked at Question Time and then Chancellor Kenneth Clarke got in on the act when he announced to the House of Commons: 'I'll tell you what I want, what I really, really want is to see healthy, sustainable growth and rising living standards for the next five years.'

John Major said on the *Today* programme that he wanted a *Spice* LP for Christmas, so we promptly biked one to Downing Street. The *Sun* did a phone-in poll and readers voted Emma for next prime minister. The fall-out continued for weeks.

We received calls from every Conservative association and fringe group in the country. Teresa Gorman invited The Girls to the House of Commons, they were invited to the House Of Lords. The late Sir James Goldsmith invited them out to dinner, stating that he found Victoria's views particularly in line with the Referendum Party. Conservatives Against A Federal Europe invited The Girls to become members, saying 'rather Spice than

Sir Michael Spicer'. The Girls were invited to countless other dinners and functions, which were all declined.

I think there was also a sense of shock from within the media: a sub-text of surprise that The Girls weren't air-headed bimbos and consternation that they had any opinions to offer at all.

If things had been busy before, the workload now trebled. As well as running the daily gauntlet of tabloid press, we now had every political commentator in the country ringing for their daily dose of Spice. The blag factor and the nutter quotient also increased proportionately.

I responded by hiding behind my voicemail. I left a deliberately long and rambling message as a barrier. My motive being that if anyone could endure that, then perhaps it really was important.

'Hello and thank you for ringing Virgin Records. If you're phoning about The Spice Girls, then I'm sorry to say The Spice Girls are unavailable for press interviews for the next six months. If you're phoning to invite them to a charity function, a film première or even the opening of an envelope, then I'm sorry to say that their diaries are completely full for the next six months. If you're calling about some of our other fabulous artistes, then I'm sorry, but I'm actually on the other line to a terribly important person, just like yourself. So please leave me a message and I'll call you back as soon as is humanly possible. Thanks very much for ringing and have a lovely day.'

The only thing was, it didn't put people off – it made them even more keen. And irritable. If you make something exclusive and unobtainable, people want it even more. If I was out of the office on a shoot all day, my mobile would be glued to my ear and when I got back to the office there would be, on an average day, at least a hundred and fifty messages.

I worried though about how many fans we had lost through the stunt. Some friends and colleagues within the media thought we'd been wrong to play ball with the *Spectator*, at the expense of losing some of our hard-earned credibility. The words swing and roundabout came to mind.

Whatever people's opinons, there was no getting away from the fact that the brief union had the desired effect of hurling The Girls even deeper into the collective consciousness and, in so doing, we sold one hell of a lot of records.

Both because of and in spite of the avalanche of publicity, Melanie C for one was extremely upset about the misrepresentation of her views.

'I'm really worried about what people at home in Liverpool are going to think. They're going to think that I'm a Tory. It's going to be, "There's that Tory Sporty Spice, from The Spice Girls. Let's get her, Tory bitch." I am seriously concerned for my personal safety when I go back to Liverpool.'

I told her she could redress the balance in subsequent interviews and that this would give them all something to talk about for the next bout of interviews.

But we still had a lot of promotion to do, so we had to put it behind us and attend to our continued duties. Later that week, we got a request from Andy Coulson to do a shoot with The Girls, photographed holding some awards that they'd won in a vote by *Sun* readers.

We arranged to meet at the Langham Hilton across the road from Broadcasting House where The Girls had been doing some radio interviews. I met Coulson downstairs, where he was cutting out some mistletoe that had been given away with that morning's paper.

'The editor thought it might be quite nice if we could do a shot under the mistletoe,' Coulson said after greeting me.

'I'll ask The Girls, Andy, you know it's up to them, mate. I'll go up and see how they're getting on, I'll be back in a minute.'

I walked up to the first floor to a suite we'd hired so that The

Girls could get their hair and make-up done for the photo. I let them know about the mistletoe request.

'I think you can take that as a No, Muff,' said Geri, beneath a cloud of powder.

'OK. Well how long before you're ready, Girls, five minutes? They want to do it in the corridor outside.'

'Yeah, in about five minutes, Muff,' said Camilla, their PA.

'Okie doke, I'll come and knock for you in five minutes, and I'll get Dave Hogan to set his lights up in the corridor now.'

'Thanks, Muff,' Camilla shouted as I left the room.

I walked back to the lobby.

'Sorry, Andy, that's a No on the mistletoe, mate.'

'Oh, well, I've just wasted twenty minutes with this then,' he said, holding up the glue and paper mistletoe.

'You never know, mate, you could always go and audition for *Blue Peter*.'

We ambled upstairs and I assisted Dave Hogan with his lights, then knocked for The Girls.

'Are we ready, ladies?'

'Yes, Muff,' came the chorused reply.

'Ooh 'ang on, I've just got to touch up my lippy,' said Geri.

Suitably touched up we strolled out into the corridor.

' 'Allo, Girls,' Coulson greeted them warmly

He then told us that he had had five copies of the awards, one for each of The Girls to hold up, but that two of them had been stolen from the office the night before and that the three that he had with him would have to be shared.

'One of you Girls can just hold your hands out pretending to hold an award and I'll get the picture desk to Mac it in.'

The Girls were standing in a row with Melanie C at one end.

' 'Ere Melanie, you just hold your hands out and pretend you're holding it up.'

'Err, no,' I intervened, 'Melanie, you share that award with

Emma, Victoria, you pretend to be holding up the award.'

How paranoid was I that Melanie C was going to be stitched up? Very!

The *People* story had only come out two days earlier and I was feeling very sensitive when it came to Melanie C. When Coulson suggested that she hold her hands out pretending to hold the award, I had these horrible visions of the *Sun* cutting her off the end of the row, and with a picture of her holding her hands out in a 'one that got away' fashion, using the photo to illustrate some follow-up story with the caption: ' "The lines were this big," said Sporty!'

Victoria stepped into the breach. When the photo was printed a few days later, nothing has been added on the Mac, and Victoria is bizarrely seen holding her hands apart.

Melanie C remained completely unaware of my fears that day. I was paranoid, yes, but where The Girls were concerned I would rather be paranoid than let them be stitched up.

When the photos were finished, we returned to the suite and The Girls then had to go to their next appointment at Capital Radio.

It was a trying day for Emma. She was extremely tired and kept breaking into tears, to be comforted by the other Girls, especially Melanie C who kept her topped up with loving hugs. She had also been feeling upset for the past few days.

The previous Sunday, Emma's first teenage sweetheart, Carlton Morgan, the first of a line of ex-boyfriends, had sold his story to the *News of the World*.

'What really hurts is the fact that I really loved him, you know. And he's just gone and destroyed a precious memory,' she said with sadness in her voice, when I offered her some sympathy the next day.

That same Monday, a *Daily Telegraph* diarist started the rumour that The Girls were going to be invited to Chequers for New Year's Eve and a couple of days later they printed a story that Lady Thatcher had sent Geri a Christmas card.

'Well, if she has, it's stuck in the post,' Geri replied when asked about it.

For a couple of weeks the *Telegraph* were never off the phone, it was obvious that they couldn't function without their daily story from Spiceworld.

The Girls were absolutely exhausted by now, they were on their last legs and were counting down the days to Sunday, the day when they would have both the Christmas Number One single and album slot, but also the day they would begin nearly three weeks' holiday – their first in over a year. A year of work-packed days and seven-day weeks. At that moment in time, they were all looking forward to their holidays more than their chart positions.

On Friday, 20 December I biked over to the *Sun* our 'insurance' exclusive from Lapland. Insurance that we didn't need after all. They were very happy.

'The editor is very pleased with it,' said Coulson. 'He said he was going to send you a little note actually,' adding with a laugh, 'Are you sure you haven't done a photo with a dummy *Mirror, Mail, Express . . .*'

'Andy, of course not,' I answered, while my mind wandered off . . . . Hmm, I wonder if we could have got away with that? Maybe next time? On the Monday, when we were Number One, The Girls had the front page and the shot was also used for a double-page poster. The *Sun*'s 'Thought For The Day?': What yule really, really want.

All we really, really want is a long rest and as I was on holiday too, I made a point of turning my phone off for two weeks. I felt I'd earned a sabbatical. I made the mistake of turning my phone on for an hour on New Year's Eve when I was expecting a call from a friend and it rang when I was having dinner with my family. It was the *News of the World*. The phone then stayed off till we returned to work on the 6 January. It had been a mad six months and I wondered what the New Year would hold for all those who inhabited Spiceworld . . .

Our return to work was enlivened by the news that 'Wannabe', which had been released in America a week earlier, had entered the Billboard Hot 100 at Number Eleven – the highest ever entry for a debut single from a British act. The Girls had even broken The Beatles' record.

The phones went berserk. It's funny, even though we thought it couldn't get any busier, or madder, the news about the imminent American chart domination threw Fleet Street into yet another frenzy. They had also found out that The Girls were going to America for a promotional tour at the end of January and the demands to accompany them were endless. Journalists phoned up demanding copies of their US itinerary, which, as I kept repeating, was confidential information. When I was out of the office, the journalists would surreptitiously try to get my assistant Nicola to fax a copy over to them. They were desperate to know what we were doing in America so that they could come out and door-step us.

Our first press engagement of the new year was with *Time* magazine, who were writing a long article for the international and US editions due to come out two weeks into release of the single in America.

I decided to use The Ritz as the location for the interview. It epitomises glamour and there is also something quintessentially English about it. I figured it would provide an interesting counterpoint to this, the *most* American of magazines. I booked a private suite and tea and cucumber sandwiches for ten people for four p.m.

On the day in question, someone at The Ritz (we suspect their press office) leaked our presence to the paparazzi. There were hordes of them outside. This actually suited us down to the ground. *Time* were early and were enjoying a drink downstairs. Present were the two writers, Maryann Bird and Julie Dam, editor Chris Redman and an executive who had flown in from New York.

The Girls arrived individually and were swept through the throng of paparazzi and through the lobby (past our friends from *Time*) with a theatrical flourish and overt sense of drama by our security guards and drivers.

The Girls looked positively radiant. They'd all got tans, they all looked rested and were a far cry from the tearful wrecks I'd said goodbye to just before Christmas.

There was something different about them. Something I couldn't quite put my finger on at first, but which became even more apparent when Melanie B arrived.

After being escorted through reception in her red velvet outfit and into the suite, she shouted out to me and Camilla Howarth: 'Could someone please ring Prada for me and ask them to stay open late. I want to do some shopping after this.'

Aaah . . . so that was it.

Money.

There must be something about receiving a large sum of money, that does wonders for your confidence and self-esteem, not to mention your innate sense of security.

This first real taste of wealth was only part of the reason they looked so radiant, generating self-assurance and a sense of a new found peace that ran concurrent with the release from financial anxiety.

Yet the sudden influx of wealth did not diminish all of the problems life threw at them and in the lift on the way up with Geri, she sighed and lamented the lack of private life she now had to suffer. She had been having a romance with a millionaire double-glazing salesman, Giovanni Laporta, whom she had been seeing over the Christmas holidays, but the *Mirror* somehow found out and had had both Geri and Laporta under twenty-four hour surveillance. They had even had journalists sifting through her rubbish in the hope of finding something revealing.

'It's just so unfair,' she said dejectedly, 'I can't even have a relationship without those people coming along and making it impossible.'

'It must be very difficult for you, Gee,' I sympathised.

'You know, they were waiting at the airport for me when I got back from my holiday, and they've been on my tail ever since. Who'd be a Spice Girl, eh?'

'Look darling, it's not going to be for ever. I know it's really difficult now, but at least you've got your mates and in a couple of years' time when all this is over you'll get your life back,' I told her, adding drily, 'You might even look back and laugh . . .' What else could I say to her? It's going to get even worse before it gets better?

'Yeah,' she said with a resigned look on her fresh and tanned face.

In a week's time Geri would cut short her relationship, destroyed by the attentions of the press. Laporta would allegedly phone both the *Sun* and the *Mirror* trying to sell his story, with both papers printing different versions. The *Sun* claimed Geri dumped him because he was two-timing her and the *Mirror* claimed Geri finished it because of 'record company pressure'. Nothing to do with the press intrusion of course, oh no. On the day the *Sun* printed their front-page story on the end of the affair, their Thought for the Day was: 2 become 1.

Later that week, Melanie B was also the victim of another kiss and tell when her ex-sweetheart Steven Mulrain shared his soul and his photo album with the *Sun*.

But for now, Melanie was enjoying herself. She brought a yellow chrysanthemum to the meeting for all The Girls, the PAs and me, swapping holiday stories with the other Girls who chatted and giggled excitedly, obviously pleased to be seeing each other again. After half an hour's catching up I brought up the team from *Time* and left them all to enjoy their tea and sandwiches.

Time were charmed by The Girls who, refreshed from their vacation and on top form, had them eating out of the palms of their manicured hands. After they had posed for a picture with the writers and signed the obligatory photos, I prepared to take Melanie B to Kettner's where she had an in interview with *Pride* magazine.

On leaving The Ritz, our Jag was waiting and we left with military precision, after one of the other Jags suddenly pulled across the road providing a makeshift barrier so that the convoy of paparazzi were unable to follow us.

On arriving at Kettner's, Melanie B waited in the car while I went to case the joint for untoward diners – just in case we'd had our appointment here leaked too and half of Fleet Street were at adjoining tables.

The management were most co-operative and gave us a table in a private room. Phew! We could relax for an hour or so. Well, I could, but Melanie had an interview to do.

Over the following two weeks, Melanie would earn the nickname Mel 'Spend, spend, spend' B. The first thing she did was buy a car for her mum – a VW Golf Cabriolet, putting down £16,000 in cash. When she'd completed the paperwork, she told the salesman, Andy Cherry, that she needed to buy a television and video recorder and, not knowing much about them, she asked him to accompany her to Selfridges to help her choose them.

As soon as he got back to the showroom after this little shopping trip, what was the first thing he did? He phoned the *Sun* and told them all about it.

'I thought she'd like the publicity,' he told the papers after his bosses took a dim view of his breaking client confidentiality and sacked him the following day when the story appeared.

The *Daily Mail* then picked up on the story, branding Melanie a 'Spite Girl' claiming she got him fired, which was untrue. It was his board of directors at Dovercourt who had given him his cards and it was nothing at all to do with Melanie.

The day after the interview with *Time* magazine, we had a photo shoot with *The Face*. We'd secured the cover of their March issue and spent all day at the shoot, which was supposed to be five individual covers of the same issue featuring a different Spice Girl but which due to logistical problems ended up featuring a picture of The Girls in their swimsuits.

Chris Heath was covering the story and he spent a lot of time over the next three weeks following The Girls around to research his story.

The shoot was at Metro Studios near Old Street. The day kicked off at midday with The Girls arriving separately over the next hour. They moaned about how it was like a new term at school, with the prospect of months of hard work ahead of them without a break, and they felt demoralised at the prospect. But it's always like that first day at school, isn't it? It takes a few days to re-engage.

The day started on a sour note for Emma, who had recently been plagued by obscene phone calls. Someone, somehow, had got hold of her mobile phone number and had been making her life a misery.

She ran from the room in floods of tears, preceded by our hair-stylist who was also enduring a bit of boyfriend trouble.

Melanie C ran out after Emma and hugged her. After a few minutes, Emma had recovered and came back into the studio. I gave her my bottle of Rescue Remedy.

'Muff thinks the answer to everything is bloody Rescue

Remedy, doesn't he?' she said half-joking to Melanie C.

I popped down to the chemist and bought bottles of Rescue Remedy for all The Girls and our hair and make-up woman. I like to buy the 20ml bottles because they're better value, but the chemist only had one of those left so I bought five 10ml bottles and one 20ml bottle.

On my return, I distributed them among The Girls, giving Emma the 20ml bottle.

'Look, you've given everyone else small bottles and I get the big one. What are you trying to say, Muff?' asked Emma, smiling, sort of.

'I tried to get big bottles for all of you, but they were sold out,' I replied as diplomatically as I could. Emma probably did need it more than the other Girls because she is more in touch with her emotions, and is the most likely to get upset and have a little weep from time to time. Victoria, however, was the least likely to need it. She was rarely upset or flustered by anything. I considered not buying her a bottle, because I didn't think she'd have much need for it, but I thought she'd feel left out if I didn't; so I did.

A little while later I went on a food run. I'd already been to the supermarket and got the drinks and the dates, but Melanie C and Emma wanted some sushi, so I grabbed Peter, one of the Music Express drivers, and we headed off to Liverpool Street Station. On the way there, my mobile phone rang. It was Thomas Quinn from the *Mirror*. Thomas worked with Matthew Wright and was a constant caller.

He wanted to know what we were doing at The Ritz the previous day. He told me there was something in that day's *Sun* about The Girls. I told him honestly that I hadn't seen what was written in the *Sun* and until I had, I couldn't comment on it. I told him I'd have to call him back.

When we got back to the studio with the sushi, one of the drivers had a copy of the *Sun* and it featured a pap picture of Geri leaving The Ritz. I didn't call Thomas Quinn back, because basically it was none of their business what we had been doing there. Despite what they may think, the papers do not have a divine right to know everything that goes on in The Girls' lives. Half an hour later, he called me back and when he asked again what The Girls were doing at The Ritz I said 'No idea, mate.'

The following day, the *Mirror* ran pictures of The Girls leaving The Ritz, accompanied by a story that said the strain was starting to show on The Spice Girls' press office: 'When asked what this latest gathering was all about, the group's hapless spokesman, Muff Fitzgerald, went blank. "I don't know; I'll call you back in thirty minutes," he stammered. As he hasn't returned one of my calls since 19 December last year, I wasn't surprised when he didn't,' they wrote.

I had made it into Matthew Wright's column. I was no longer a nobody.

The Face photo shoot continued without further incident. Chris Heath took each of The Girls off into a corner to interview them individually. Towards the end of the shoot, the photographer, ignoring protocol, went into the dressing room to ask The Girls if they would slip into some flesh-coloured bikinis and do a shot that would make them appear naked.

The answer was a resounding no. It had been a very long day, The Girls were tired and they did not like the idea one little bit. They'd been virtually naked all day anyway, with Geri declaring at one point that everyone else in the room had to get their kit off to join The Girls in the spirit of the occasion.

The following day was the first day of the video shoot for 'Mama'. A huge studio space had been hired in Perivale, west London on the way to Heathrow. About five sets had been built in front of tiered seating, which was to accommodate around five hundred children and their parents.

At this stage, the shooting script for the video had a game

show theme with The Girls hosting something similar to *Noel's House Party.*

I arrived early and The Girls were already there preparing their costumes and sitting through what would be hours upon hours of hair and make-up. It was bitterly cold down on the set, although the dressing rooms had heaters and were warm.

There was a flurry of activity everywhere with electricians laying cables, carpenters building sets, men with paintbrushes wandering around dabbing here and there, technicians holding up light meters, caterers walking in with boxes of fruit and veg.

My function was twofold. I was there to chaperone Chris Heath, to make sure he was getting the access he wanted to, give him any information he required and to generally make sure he was happy. Secondly, I also had to make sure The Girls were happy while Chris was there and they didn't feel pressured or put-upon in any way. I had to strike a fine balance and try to keep both parties happy. Chris likes to spend as much time as possible with the people he is writing about, and he really enjoys being a part of what is going on. However, The Girls do not feel comfortable with 'fly on the wall' type assignments and had asked that Chris didn't hang out in the dressing room, especially as they would have their families with them over the next two days, with their mothers all due to appear in the video. The Girls were all feeling very jumpy, because their families had been constantly intimidated by the press and photographers. While I was on set, my primary task was to meet The Girls' needs at all times.

Another task over the next few days was to assist photographer Ray Burmiston in setting up some more 'Kodak moments', which we would use for press purposes when 'Mama' was released on March 3. Either Ray or I would shout 'Kodak moment' and get The Girls to strike a pose for posterity.

Not long after our arrival, a group of paparazzi turned up outside and started taking photographs of The Girls through the glass entrance, as they moved between set and dressing rooms on the first floor. We got busy ripping up bin bags and taping them over the glass to allow us some privacy. The police refused to move them on, however, saying they had just as much right to stand on the pavement as anyone else.

I went to the supermarket to get some sparkling mineral water, Diet Coke, fresh fruit and dates and on my return I discovered the mums had arrived. I walked into the dressing room to discover a woman with blonde hair in her underwear. Embarrassed, I apologised, left, and brought the shopping in a few minutes later when she gave me the all clear.

I was introduced to Jackie, Victoria's mum – who was now dressed – Vic's sister Louise, Andrea, Melanie B's mother, Joan, Melanie C's Ma and Paul, her brother, and Geri's mum, Anna-Maria.

Victoria told me that her ex-fiancé, Mark Wood, had been followed and harassed by the *People* that morning. I offered to talk to him. She got him on the phone and he told me that a photographer had surreptitiously taken his photograph and he was door-stepped by a journalist demanding to know intimate details of their former relationship.

'Listen, I love Victoria,' he told me, 'and I would never do anything to hurt her.'

I advised him just to say 'No comment' and to shut the front door in their faces if he got door-stepped again. And to say the same thing if he got telephone calls from any journalists.

'Just say no comment, that's all you can do, mate. But if they come into your garden or are on your property, then you can phone the police who will move them on, but they can't do anything if they're sitting outside your house waiting on the pavement.'

A few months later, following a throwaway comment by Victoria during a television show, when she said that she'd finished with him but kept the ring, Mark felt extremely hurt and responded by selling his story to the *Sun*.

Hunter from the *Gladiators* was making a cameo appearance in the video and lifted Geri above his head for one of our 'Kodak moments'. Geri was wearing a pair of heat-sensitive trousers, which changed colour the warmer they got. After Hunter put Geri down you could see his handprints showing exactly where he had been holding her. She had a hand-print on her bum.

Hunter and I shared a cup of tea in the canteen, when we swopped media intrusion horror stories. At this time he was going out with Ulrika Johnson and he had had more than his fair share of paparazzi hi-jinks. In a couple of months' time their relation-ship would end, and his solution to evade the photographers camped outside his house would be to leave the house with a cardboard box over his head.

The children were brought in and took their places in the tiered seating that faced the set. Priscilla, The Girls' choreogra-pher, led them through a series of complicated dance moves and hand gestures they were to perform on cue from their seats. The air of anticipation was palpable. The audience had been waiting in a marquee outside for two hours, eating hamburgers in an effort to stave off the sub-zero temperatures.

The assistant stage manager told them he was going to bring The Spice Girls down in five minutes. Screams and child-like cheers echoed round the huge studio.

'Before I bring them down, I want to remind everybody that no photographs are allowed. If anyone is seen with a camera, they will be immediately told leave. There will be no exceptions,' he told the crowd.

The floor manager, spikey-haired Barry Ashworth, who spends the rest of his life playing in a band called the Dub Pistols, went to collect The Girls.

A colossal roar greeted the Fab Five as, waving and blowing kisses, they took up their positions in front of the crowd.

'Hiya! Is everybody all right?'

'YEEEEEEEEEEEEEEEEEEEEEEEEEESSSSSSSSSSS!' was the shrill and hysterical answer.

'Thanks for coming, sorry about all the waiting around,' said Mel C through her radio mike.

'Right, silence please,' shouted the ASM. 'Everybody in their places.'

The five Spice Girls stood in a line facing the tiered seating and did a straight run through of 'Mama', the little boys and girls in the audience gazing down admiringly, mouthing every word, while trying to follow the hand-jive that Priscilla was leading them through by the side of the set.

After five takes, the director yelled cut, and the ASM told The Girls to have a break and the crowd not to worry because The Girls would be back soon. As mothers took their toddlers to queue for the toilets during this interval, I got one of the drivers to take me to Tesco's for more drinks and fresh fruit salad.

On my return, I handed packets of the fruit salad to The Girls.

'Oh Muff, I don't want anything at the moment, all right?' said Melanie C, suddenly upset. 'If you'd just found out what I've found out—' she trailed off and pushed past me, leaving the room, obviously in a state of shock.

Melanie had just discovered she had a sister she never knew about. When her parents separated, her dad, Alan Chisholm, had had a baby, Emma, by someone else and they had lost touch.

The *Sun* found out about Emma, and told Alan to tell Melanie about her, otherwise they would. Hence Alan's call to Mel today. She was completely gobsmacked. The other Girls were very supportive, but, like all of the other little bombshells that were constantly going off all around them, this one had to be put to one side for the moment and that day's Spice Girls' agenda dealt with first.

Fifteen minutes later Melanie was on set going through her paces again for the cameras. She was a true professional. Like all of The Girls, she had a resilience that was an essential ingredient for those increasingly frequent days when it seemed the whole world was involved in a conspiracy to get them.

Chapter Six

• •

ON TOP OF THE
WORLD, MAMA!

New York City, January 1997

Screeeeeeeeeeeeeech! Five Spice Girls, their security guards, PAs and I were thrown violently from our seats in the Previa that swerved up on to the pavement, the driver slamming on his brakes to avoid the paparazzi photographer who had jumped out right in front of our moving vehicle, nearly killing all of us in the process.

The shopping went everywhere. Barney's, Prada and Tiffany bags all flying through the air.

This was the signal for four other photographers, who had been doggedly pursuing us all morning, to leap out of their car and start taking pictures through the windows as the stunned and dishevelled Girls picked themselves up off the floor.

But they hadn't reckoned on New York's Finest.

A detective, who, in order to preserve his anonymity we will call Officer Tony Capelli, jumped out of the van, and reached for his badge, in the process revealing the regulation side-arm that every officer in the NYPD carries for protection.

'Put your hands up against the side of the vehicle,' he hollered in his most direct DON'T EVEN DREAM OF MESSING WITH ME! voice; his accent thicker than his Momma's clam chowder, quickly and expertly frisking the first photographer for concealed weapons. At the same time his colleague, a veritable giant of a man, whom we'll call Detective Jim O'Sullivan, was doing the same to the other four paparazzi perps who were now lined up by the side of their car.

'Are you aware that I could arrest you all not only for harassment, but for deliberately trying to cause an accident and in so doing endangering human life, which as a Federal offence carries a minimum five year sentence?' he enquired pointedly. 'You ever thought about what the inside of Ryker's Island looks like? Eh, Buddy?'

Our saviour Tony let the pack go with a warning that if he spotted them on our tail or anywhere near The Spice Girls again, they'd be arrested and charged with harassment.

We were in New York for the second time in as many months. The first time, in November, The Spice Girls were unheard of. They were complete unknowns and could stroll the sidewalks unrecognised and unmolested.

'We love New York,' Mel C told me at the 'Mama' video shoot, before we left the UK. 'America is the last place where we can walk around and no one bothers us.'

Not this time, sweetheart. No. When we arrived The Girls were number four on the Billboard Hot 100 with 'Wannabe', after having moved up from their record-breaking chart entry of eleven.

Consequently, they were hotter than a jacket potato stuffed with vindaloo and were pursued with fervent determination by a pack of paparazzi photographers and tabloid stringers each time their platformed heels left the luxurious haven of the Four Seasons Hotel. Hence the need for the two private detectives we had brought with us from Britain to implement The Girls' personal security.

Although The Girls had been granted instant celebrity status in America, they had yet to be admitted into New York Society. But right then, they definitely didn't have time to socialise. Their schedule was full from dawn to dusk and beyond. So there wasn't much of that classic New York inter-celebrity mingling. Yet. That would come when they performed on *Saturday Night Live* with Rob Lowe and Robert De Niro in a few months from then. De Niro would ask The Girls to dinner.

Prior to flying to New York, Simon Fuller had already been aware of the shift of celebrity status The Girls had enjoyed. 'We really have to watch it in America this time around,' he told me at a meeting in London just before we left. 'You know anything could happen.' In New York anything is possible.

While partly revelling in the prospect of fevered attention, The Girls were also quite depressed because they did love to go shopping when they were in New York and this situation made it very difficult. In actual fact, doing anything in New York had become a logistical nightmare.

Especially when one's task was to organise a discreet photo shoot on top of the Empire State Building. The purpose of the shoot was to get pictures to feed to the world's press when 'Wannabe' reached its impending top position in a couple of weeks' time.

The shoot would involve The Girls draping a Union Jack over the edge of the observation tower on the eighty-ninth floor while our photographer for this trip, Liz Johnson-Artur, bravely leaned out of a helicopter hovering in sub-zero temperatures a few hundred feet away. The helicopter pilot, Al Cerullo – the man who did all the stunts for the Empire State Building sequences in *Sleepless in Seattle* – would repeatedly buzz the building with an enthusiasm not seen since Robert Duvall led his squad of chopper-friendly men in *Apocalypse Now*. By the time of the shoot on Wednesday lunchtime, we'd have had a surplus of 'The horror', the only thing missing being the music of the 'Ride of The Valkyries' and the smell of napalm.

Try keeping the organisation of this little stunt a secret!

I flew in on Sunday 26 January accompanied by Chris Heath who wanted more material for his *Face* feature. As in England, Chris was after as much access as possible, while the management wanted to give him as little as they would get away with. My job was to mediate between the two parties, trying to keep both sides happy and ensure that the feature happened.

On arriving at the Peninsula Hotel, Chris went out for dinner with friends and I crawled into bed. I had caught flu on the set of the 'Mama' video and it was kicking in quite badly. Despite my illness, I was up at five the next morning, partly with jet lag but mainly because the phone had already started ringing.

In New York, you invariably do a day's work before you go down to breakfast, all those magazine editors in Britain are up and at it and calls had to be made about shoots and interviews we were going to do when we got back, even before I addressed the tasks that awaited my attention in the Big Apple.

However, since I was not meeting Simon Fuller and The Girls until lunchtime, that gave me the time to attend to a personal matter of the utmost importance.

The Tommy Hilfiger coat that I'd bought when I was in New York with The Girls in November had let me down badly. I'd worn the coat every day since November and it had served me well, keeping me and, on occasions various Spice Girls, as warm as toast. Three days before the trip, I'd taken it to the dry cleaners but when I went to collect it I almost cried. The colours had run and it was now a dirty pink colour – a little like Divine's hair colour in *Pink Flamingos*.

Fuelled by my indignation, I was at Macy's at ten a.m. when they opened on that crisp, bright, New York Monday morning.

Making my way to the cash desk, I presented the coat for inspection, my indignation tempered by the realisation that I had not kept my receipt and, without it, the chance of gaining some satisfaction did not look too good. The guy at the cash desk started giving me the bum's rush.

And then an angel appeared.

'Hi there!' A high-pitched Noo Yawk accent cut through the intransigent air. I turned around and there was Marcia (it said so on her lapel badge), the lovely assistant who had served me two months before.

'Hello love! How are you?'

'I'm fine, thank you. How are you?'

'Well, not too good really, I've got flu actually, but hey, you remember me, right?' I said loudly, alerting not only the people behind the cash desk but probably everyone on the first floor.

'Oh sure, you were so excited when you bought that coat.'

'Thank you!' I cried, aiming the words at the guy behind the cash desk like a steel-tipped arrow. 'She remembers me. Hooray.'

I explained that the colours of the coat that I loved had run. Marcia was sympathetic but told me that they had sold out of that design a month ago. Oh damn.

'But you know what,' she continued reassuringly, 'Tommy's in store today, maybe he can help.'

'Excuse me?' I replied, a little stunned but with a presence of celebrity glow starting to creep through my body, like the time I met Donny and Marie Osmond at the Fender Soundhouse in Tottenham Court Road when I was eleven years old.

'Tommy's in store.'

'Oh well, I'll just wait for Tommy then,' I said with a display of mock-nonchalance.

Five minutes later, Marcia said matter offactly: 'Here's Tommy.'

And she was right. Surrounded by six of Macy's suits and sporting a blue cashmere blazer, white chinos, penny loafers and an apple-pie smile, into the department strolled America's foremost designer.

'Tommy!' I yelled in my best blagger's-oh-yes-I-am-most-definitely-English-and-a-class-turn-mate accent.

I approached with a smile on my face and my hand held out in a gesture of introduction and friendship.

The smile left his face, to be replaced by a look of intense anxiety. I could almost read his mind.

'Oh no, who is this crazy guy? Remember the Dakota Building . . . Oh-oh!'

The suits around him stiffened, while he flinched and dropped back behind them. I pushed my way through, coming on like Rupert Pupkin in *The King Of Comedy*.

'Tommy,' I bullhorned. 'Tommy, Muff Fitzgerald, Virgin Records. I'm the publicist for The Spice Girls.'

His body language changed immediately, the tension evaporated like a bowl of freebase, he grinned and all the Macy's men sycophantly smiled in tandem.

'Oh The Spice Girls? What happened to them? I thought I was going to dress them?'

'Tommy, they've been so busy. As you know, they've been number one in thirty countries around the world and they've been working non-stop.'

'Are they here now?'

'Ooh, they certainly are, Tommy. We're over here for a week to do promotion. Their single "Wannabe" is at number four on the Billboard Hot 100 and it's going to be Number One within a week or two.'

'I'd really like to dress them,' said Tommy.

'Oh, Tommy, I'm sure The Girls would love to be dressed by

you. They love your clothes, man. Every time we come over they always take back a little bit of Hilfiger.'

'Are you doing any photo sessions while you're here in New York?'

'Well, actually, we are doing a session on top of the Empire State Building in a couple of days, Tommy.'

'I'd love to dress them for that. Where are you staying?'

'Well, The Girls are at the Four Seasons, but I'm at the Peninsula – I'm over here with a journalist from *The Face*,' I said, quickly explaining that journalists never stay in the same hotel as The Girls.

Tommy's face lit up.

'*The Face*? Can I dress them for that?'

'Oh Tommy, I'm sorry, we've already done the photo session for *The Face*, but I'm sure The Girls would love some of your stuff to keep them warm on the top of the Empire State Building,' I said, continuing earnestly. 'But listen, Tommy, I'm really sorry to lay this on you right now. But you see this coat. I love this coat. And I got it dry cleaned the other day and look what happened: all the colours have run.'

Tommy looked concerned and not a little embarrassed in front of the suits.

'Well, ask them to change it,' he suggested.

'I already have, Tommy, and they said they're out of stock.'

'OK, here's what we'll do,' he said, rising to this impromptu sense of occasioned blaggery. 'Go over there and choose any coat, that's on me; I'll get my people to locate another coat like that from our warehouse and we'll send it directly to your hotel. And let me put you in touch with my head of publicity and we'll arrange for The Girls to come to our showroom and choose whatever they like.'

I thanked him profusely and he led me over to some excruciatingly bright silver puffas and said: 'You like this coat? Goldie wore this one for the MTV awards, here, try it on.'

Slipping into the coat had the effect of making me feel like an ornament on a Christmas tree. The material was bright silver and made up of tiny holograms that refracted the light into a thousand dazzling particles. It cost $700 and it was actually a tad too ostentatious for me. Tommy went to the phone to get hold of his PR people.

I asked one of the assistants to unlock a quieter garment. Tommy was writing down some information with a thick black marker when he beckoned me back to the cash desk. 'Where did you say you're staying again?' he asked.

'The Peninsula, Tommy.' I was still wearing Goldie's jacket. Tommy suddenly spun me round on my side and with a dramatic flourish, autographed the label that adorned the side of the coat. Oh. I guess I'm keeping this one then.

'Whoah! Hey thanks ever so much, Tommy,' I said, adding only half-jokingly, 'I'll never wash it, mate.'

'That'll be a collector's item, man,' one of his aides said admiringly.

'You're not kidding, mate,' I replied. Collecting dust in my wardrobe.

I promised to call his PR and floated out of Macy's to tell The Girls, Simon Fuller and Chris Health of my lucky encounter.

'That could only happen to you, Muff,' said Simon over lunch at the Four Seasons a little while later. 'When you go to the showroom, don't forget to pick out a black puffa for me.'

'I'm sure that won't be a problem, Simon,' I replied, before we got down to fine-tuning our week in New York.

He allocated Wednesday lunchtime for the shoot at the Empire State Building and then decided what access to give Chris Heath. He said Chris could accompany The Girls that evening on a bus which New York radio station Z100 would fill with competition winners and as the itinarary stated:

The Girls will board an English double-decker bus along with afternoon personality (and music director) 'Cubby' and ten to fifteen contest winners for a tour of Manhattan. They will stop at specific locations and provide continuous Live on air remotes with Z100 every ten to fifteen minutes. The idea is to create the illusion on air that they are having a party all over the city. The Girls will be expected to be enthusiastic on each remote broadcast and interact with the DJ and the contest winners

We thought they might be doing an interview with Howard Stern. Simon said Chris could accompany The Girls to that interview but he didn't want him to go to the photo shoot on the Empire State Building.

'It's too public, Muff. Just in case anything goes wrong,' he said. I said nothing for the moment, but I made a note to try and persuade Simon otherwise, later.

After lunch, I headed back to the Peninsula to let Chris know what access Simon had decided. My phone rang. It was a stringer for the *Mirror*.

'Oh hi, is that Muff Fitzgerald?'

'Yes.'

'I'm a reporter out here for the *Daily Mirror*.'

'Right.'

'I understand you're planning to do a photo shoot on the Empire State Building this week.'

'Who told you that?'

'Oh word gets around, you know.'

'Well, we were, but it turned out to be a logistical nightmare,' I said, rapidly constructing a smokescreen. 'No, now we're going to be doing a session on USS *Intrepid*, the aircraft carrier, instead.'

'Oh, that's a really good idea, I can see my headline now. ALL THE SPICE GIRLS LOVE A SAILOR! Can I come along and do an interview and take some photos please?'

'Listen, why don't you give me your number, and when I know exactly what time we're doing it, I'll give you a ring and let you know, OK?' I fibbed.

The journalist gave me her number. We did not want any press present at our photo shoot because it would spoil the exclusivity of the shots, before we had decided where we were going to place them and also, it was somewhat premature, because we would not be Number One in the States for a week or two.

After I put the phone down, I pondered on how this stringer could have tracked me down and found out about our plans for the photo session. I was registered at the hotel under the name Edgar Broughton. I found out a few days later that while we were having lunch in the Four Seasons, we were being staked out and ear-wigged by stringers for three British newspapers and a couple of paparazzi who had the tables nearest our own in the fruitful hope of gleaning as much information as possible.

Then I was followed back to my hotel.

I had been feeling quite paranoid of late, but now things were really starting to get out of hand.

I phoned the Empire State Building office and asked them to lie if any journalists, British or otherwise, phoned and asked if we were doing a photo shoot. They were most unhelpful.

'We're not your press office,' the woman told me flatly.

I explained that we'd been subjected to the unwelcome attentions of tabloid journalists and I was only trying to protect my artists. Anyway, we were paying them a lot of money to shoot there, so the least they could do was be a bit more helpful. They then said they would not restrict access to the press while we were shooting. It was a public place and they had a perfect right to be there. It was suggested that if we wanted to shoot without the press present, they would be prepared to let us do it at eight a.m., before they let the public in. I said I would find out if we could do that.

That afternoon, while The Girls were being interviewed and photographed by *Entertainment Weekly*, I took a cab with Camilla Howarth down to the Hilfiger showrooms to arrange blagging some clobber for The Girls. They later sent over five wardrobe-sized boxes of clothes to their hotel.

Before we left the Four Seasons, I showed The Girls a photo session for them to approve, shot by Ray Burmistion on the set of the 'Mama' video.

After Camilla and I left the Hilfiger showrooms, arranging to meet on the Z100 bus later that evening, I did a little shopping and made my way back to the hotel. On reaching my room, I suddenly broke into a hot sweat: severe palpitations shuddered through my body. I was having a heart attack. And I'm totally not kidding already.

Oh my God! The photo session. Where was it? Damn. I had just lost a five grand, irreplaceable photo session. Packed with magic once-in-a-lifetime moments. The Girls with their mums on the video set. I was about to become Mr Not Very Popular At All.

Dashing out of my room, I retraced my steps, stopping at reception and every shop down Broadway where I'd been flashing my plastic. My paranoia ran with me, rampant. In a camera shop where I'd bought some film, I was sure the guy behind the counter was lying. He had the photos, I was sure of it. He knew The Girls were Number Four on the Billboard chart. He knew the British newspapers would pay a fortune for these photos of The Girls with their mums. Whaddya mean I didn't leave anything in your shop, mate? Behind that smile lay a smug self-assurance at all the readies he was about to shake down. I just knew it. Are you sure you didn't see anything?

Thoroughly dejected, I headed back to the hotel. If I hadn't left the photos in the camera shop, or at any of the other shops, or at the hotel reception, then only the very worst thing was possible. I had left them in a cab.

I drank half a bottle of Rescue Remedy and went to call Chris Heath, as we had to get ready to go on the bus.

Chris was an absolute sweetheart. So supportive and full of good suggestions. He suggested we check the Four Seasons, where I originally had the session and he conversed at length with the receptionist, head of security and the man in the men's room, where I had earlier been pummelling the porcelain. If they had come across the sesh, we would find out.

After searching everywhere, Chris then found the number for Yellow Taxi's lost property saying: 'Listen, Muff, if Nick Parks could find Wallace and Gromit after leaving them in a taxi here, then I'm sure you're going to get your photos back. Come on let's find a bar and have a drink before we get on the bus.'

Feeling dejected, but buoyed up by Chris's support and optimism we waited for the bus at a Mexican bar and munched on a couple of enchiladas while we anticipated The Girls' arrival.

The English double-decker has been transmogrified into a single-decker coach packed with a lot of very drunk people by the time we climbed on board to join the merry pranksters. The beer was flowing and The Girls were chatting away to the competition winners, most of whom had never heard of The Spice Girls and were equally as unfamiliar with their music. Every ten minutes or so we went live to the studio and 'Cubby' would hand a mobile phone to one of The Girls who'd chatter animatedly into it.

'Hello, Noo Yaaaaaaaawk!' screamed Geri, 'I'll tell you what I want, what I really, really want. I wish you were all here with us on the Z100 love bus, people, we are having such a wicked party!'

Victoria was suffering badly with the flu. Her nose was blocked, she kept coughing and was running a temperature of 104. But she is a sterling professional.

'Hello, New York, I can't believe you're not at this party!' she said, sounding as though she was the life and soul of the party of her life. As soon as she handed the phone back to the DJ, she looked over at Chris and me, once again looking ill and sounding bunged up, and said drily: 'It's not the Number Ones, you know,' gesturing with her hands at the drunken and tiresome scene unfolding around her, '*This* is the highlight.'

The wheels kept turning and the winners got more and more drunk. We kept stopping off at various locations for more food, drinks and back-rubs. One woman started trying to cop off with Richard, one of our security men. Geri suddenly decided she wanted to have a go at driving the bus. A fully-laden passenger bus in rush-hour Manhattan traffic. But what the lady wants, the lady gets. The driver complied.

Be afraid, be very afraid.

I could already see the headlines in the following day's *New York Post*: 'SPICE GIRLS' CARNAGE IN MID-TOWN PILE UP!' I lamented the lack of seat belts on the vehicle. But Geri took to it like a duck to wet stuff. A bit of a natural, in fact, pulling up a few blocks from the Four Seasons where The Girls' Previa was waiting for its famous charges. We were off the bus.

I had a sleepless night thinking about the lost photo session, wondering if it would turn up in the morning. I met Chris in the lobby at six a.m. We were going with The Girls to WKTU, an R'n'B radio station based out in Jersey City. The Girls were special guests on Ru Paul's breakfast show. This was in place of the Howard Stern show.

Chris and I were in the reception of the Four Seasons at six fifteen waiting for The Girls to emerge, supping a tea 'to go' and munching one of those New York donuts shaped like a penis.

The radio plugger turned up. She was a little bit sniffy, to say the least. She was into R-a-w-k and it was apparent from her attitude that she thought The Spice Girls were of less substance than the froth gathered on her early morning cup of coffee.

The Girls came down, weary at that ungodly hour, but prepared to work. Not unsurprisingly, they wanted to get some breakfast on the way. The plugger told us we would be late if we stopped but we insisted that we at least stop for some coffee, bagels and muffins for The Girls.

The vibes were not good.

On arrival at WKTU, we were ushered into the studio. Ru Paul came out to greet us, talking in a fake cockney accent. He doesn't wear drag for his radio show and was wearing a black shirt, black jeans and a black Stetson. His legs go on forever. He seemed very pleased to see The Girls. I introduced Chris as a journalist from *The Face*.

'Oh my god not *The Face*,' he said, 'I hate *The Face*.'

Chris and I sort of smiled nervously, not sure if he was joking or not.

We all went into the studio where his show was going out live.

The Girls sat at the desk and put their headphones on. Chris and I sat on the floor, unobtrusively, Chris as ever taking notes in the large notebook that goes everywhere with him. The atmosphere was relaxed and Ru Paul was funny.

But suddenly during the commercial break, while they were chatting away, Ru Paul suddenly freaked out.

'There's that *Face* guy writing down everything I say. Who's from the management here? I want you to kick that guy out of the studio NOW!'

At first Chris and I thought he was joking and that it was part of the Ru Paul act.

He was being serious.

'Why?' asked Geri.

'Because it's stinking old eighties' thinking,' he said, giving his paranoid thoughts on the magazine.

Chris and I got up and left the studio.

In the van on the way back to Manhattan, the atmosphere

was subdued and weary. We stopped for some soft drinks and then went straight to the Museum of Television and Radio where The Girls' morning interview schedule looked like this:

9:00 a.m. KDWB, Minneapolis, Minnesota
9:30 a.m. WWZZ, Washington, DC
9:40 a.m. WPRO, Providence, Rhode Island
9:50 a.m. WXXL, Orlando, Florida
10:00 a.m. KMXV, Kansas City, Missouri
10:10 a.m. WWKX, Providence, Rhode Island
10:20 a.m. KKFR, Phoenix, Arizona
10:40 a.m. WAPE, Jacksonville, Florida
11:00 a.m. KHKS, Dallas, Texas
11:20 a.m. WRVQ, Richmond, Virginia
11:30 a.m. KLUC, Las Vegas, Nevada
11:40 a.m. KLLC, San Francisco
11:50 a.m. KHTS, San Diego, California

After saying 'Good Morning America!' non-stop for three hours all The Girls wanted to do was get the XXXX out of there for a quick munch before an afternoon of non-stop magazine interviews.

When I got back to my room, the phone was ringing. It was the woman from the *Mirror*. She was in reception with a photographer.

Would I like to come down for a coffee? No, I would not. Making my excuses, I decided not to answer the phone in my room and to work off the voicemail facility and leave the hotel via the service exit so that I wouldn't be followed. She was at the wrong hotel anyway. She'd have been better off stalking The Girls at the Four Seasons, but I imagined she felt it was less daunting following me, as I didn't have armed police with me to send her on her way. And it was inevitable that eventually I would lead her to The Girls.

I made my way to the Yellow Taxi lost property office. A man who could have been Travis Bickle's younger brother was manning the reception area. Any optimism I had maintained was quickly dashed when he claimed that I'd have more chance of winning the lottery than finding the photos. Twice. I headed back to the hotel and decided to bite the pillow and let Camilla Howarth know I'd slipped up.

I phoned her.

'Camilla.'

'Hi, Muff.'

'Listen, Camilla, I've got to tell you something, you know the 'Mama' photo session. Well I—'

'Yeah, I've got it here in my room—'

'What! Oh THANK YOU SO MUCH, CAMILLA!!! You know I thought I'd left it in a cab after we went to Tommy Hilfiger yesterday. I have been all over New York searching for it. Thank you so much.'

'Muff, you idiot, you should have said something. I put it in my room yesterday at the Four Seasons to keep it safe.'

Thank goodness for that then. I felt a tremendous sense of relief.

I spent the rest of the day finalising arrangements for the shoot at the Empire State Building.

I went with Richard Harvey, our private detective and security representative, to meet the security adviser for the Empire State Building. It was just like planning a presidential visit. We walked through and timed the whole route – from arrival at the back door, going up in the service elevator and transferring to the main elevator at the eighty-fifth floor, to which areas were going to be cordoned off, how many men would be present, what colour underwear they would be wearing and what they would all eat for breakfast. All the while Richard took fastidious notes in a little book. He used to be a police officer and was very good at taking down particulars, though he opted out of that function with the drunk lady on the Z100 bus.

Simon had decided that he didn't want The Girls to get up early to do the photo shoot before the public were admitted, because The Girls had been up at six thirty nearly every morning since they'd been in New York and he wanted them to have a lie-in. The plan was to shoot from two p.m. for half an hour.

I was feeling quite anxious that morning. I was worried that hordes of reporters would find out the time we were doing the shoot and come along and spoil our exclusives. I got a cab down to the Heliport at West 30th Street on the Hudson River.

The sky was clear and a deep blue. It was bitterly cold. We waited for the chopper to arrive. I was there to pay Al Cerullo and get a walkie-talkie which would enable me to issue directions when he was fluttering above us. I left a very brave Liz Johnson-Artur (she would be dangling out of the chopper on a tiny harness) and Nikki Chapman, who was chaperoning a camera-man from GMTV, to get in the chopper while I got a cab back to the Empire State Building.

I got back just as The Girls arrived at the back door. We were ushered in amid a swell of muscle. The wind howled through the building down the lift shafts and it was quite freezing inside, never mind outside.

As we went up in the lift I briefed The Girls on what we would be doing when we reached the top. We reached the observation tower and I took The Girls over to the railings where they would hold out the flags towards the helicopter. They stood in a line and I got them to pose with a Union Jack first. We stood there freezing, scouring the skies for a sign of our helicopter.

I told The Girls to look in the direction of the helicopter.

'Hello, Al. Come in, Al . . . . Are you receiving me, Al . . . . Over.'

I couldn't get contact with the chopper. Where was he? What was going on?

Ten minutes passed. There was no sign of him. The walkie-talkie wasn't working. I wondered if there had been a technical problem of some kind.

The Girls went inside to warm up. After another ten anxious minutes the walkie-talkie crackled into life.

'Err, hello, Muff, this is Al calling, come in, Muff . . . Over'

'Al, man, where are you, what's happening?'

'Sorry about the slight delay, we were refused clearance by JFK, had to wait to get the air-space allotted. We're on our way . . . should be with you in five minutes . . . over . . .'

'Message received and understood, Al, over.'

'And hey Al . . . over.'

'What . . . over.'

'Remember, Charlie don't surf . . . Over.'

I ran inside to get The Girls.

I bumped into Chris Heath. Simon had finally relented after I had badgered him and he had allowed Chris to attend.

He was angry.

'Muff, where have you been? I've been waiting for you downstairs at the entrance for the last half an hour. There was a huge queue of people and they wouldn't let me up.'

'I'm so sorry, Chris. I thought we said we'd meet up here.'

'No, we arranged to meet downstairs at the front entrance at one thirty.'

'I'm really sorry, Chris.'

'It's just that I haven't been given that much access to The Girls and when I am, this happens . . . It's really frustrating.'

I felt bad about this, but at that moment I couldn't give it any further thought. I went to gather my precious charges.

'Right, come on, the chopper's on its way,' I yelled at The Girls. 'OK, ladies, could you take your places please, thank you.

Where's Emma? Emma! Come on, love. It's not going to take long, we'll all be back in the warm before we know it. Thank you.'

I tried to boost their freezing and flagging morale. 'Listen everyone, think of The Beatles. This is an historic shot. Wave to the helicopter. You're on top of the world.'

The helicopter came in alongside and The Girls started gesticulating wildly. The woman from the Empire State Building had said that the chopper was allowed to come in no closer than five hundred metres. If it came any closer and there was a sudden strong gust of wind, we would be looking at a different sort of headline the next day.

'How's it going, Al? . . . Is Liz happy . . . Over.'

'She's changing film . . . over.'

'Tell me when she's ready for me to change flags . . . over.'

We were going to do one lot of shots with a Union Jack and then shoot a few rolls with The Girls holding a Stars and Stripes.

'Listen,' Al said, 'we're not close enough. I need to come in a couple of hundred feet more. Can you stall the Empire State people while I do that?'

'You got it, Al . . . Over.' I hollered in my best huh-I'm-in-the-Marine-Corps-voice.

I created a diversion.

The woman from the Empire State Building had said before we began, that if we were going to use the American Flag for our session, it had to be an authentic flag and at no time could it touch the ground. I absent-mindedly dropped it on the ground.

She totally freaked out already.

'You've dropped our flag on the ground. You promised not to do that . . . I can't believe you've done that . . . you show some respect,' she said bending over, holding the flag to her bosom like a newborn baby and lovingly folding the unfurled material.

'Go, Al,' I whisper into my handset. He zoomed in and The Girls gave it all they could.

Coming up from folding the flag, the woman started to really freak out: 'Tell him he's gotta get back NOW! There could be a serious accident. Tell him he's gotta get back or we stop everything now.'

'I'm so sorry,' I said deadpan. 'Al, apparently you're too close, mate, could you get back a bit?'

As he moved back I swapped flags, dropping the Union Jack to the ground in my haste. This time no one said a word.

As it was the middle of the day, the place was packed with tourists. And what do tourists always have with them? Yes. A camera. And they were all busy snapping away. It was nigh on impossible to make sure that all the 'tourists' were bona fide and weren't professional photographers. It was a nightmare.

On top of that, there was a TV crew from GMTV on the tower with us. The sound man had a huge boom microphone which he kept pointing in The Girls' direction. I had to keep asking him to stand back and get out of shot.

I asked him nicely, but firmly, three times. He ignored me. I lost it.

'Listen mate, just get out of the way, will you? Get that microphone out of here. You're completely ruining our session, all right?'

The Girls exchanged glances. Geri, a little shocked said: 'I wouldn't like to get on the wrong side of you, Muff.'

I felt bad that I'd lost control in front of the artists, but I was really stressed out there. We only had one go at this shoot and if politeness fails, well, then sometimes you have to become blunt. We had spent a lot of money setting this up, and I was not prepared to let some TV technician ruin it all.

We got the call that Liz had got enough. Then the woman from the Empire State Building told me we owed them another

$2,000 because we'd gone over time. I paid her and we made our way back through the crowd of rubber-necking tourists to the lift.

There was a tense atmosphere in the lift on the way down. There was that awkwardness that is often present after someone has expressed their anger. The Girls appeared resentful towards me.

Chris was also annoyed with me. But I was only human, after all. I was doing the best job I could, under trying and extremely stressful circumstances.

We left the building, The Girls, Simon and the phalanx of security piled into the Previa and went back to the hotel. Chris and I would meet them there after we had gone back to the heliport to pick up our photographer.

On arrival at the hotel, Chris was going to interview The Girls, who really would rather have been shopping.

'Ohh Muff,' Victoria moaned, 'he's had more time than all the others put together. I want to go and get some Saks.' Victoria had a Saks store card she wanted to put to good use.

'Listen, it's just the way he works, Vee,' I explained. 'If Chris says he needs the time, he needs the time. He's extremely thorough.'

As I left him in Victoria's suite with the other four Girls, I made my way upstairs to Simon Fuller's room for an impromptu crisis conference.

News has just come in from London that was going to keep me more than busy over the next few days and would stretch my fast failing grip on reality to the limit.

Chapter Seven

MIAMI VICE . . . !

Miami, 31st, January 1997

Ilyana Silanovich had the type of looks that could drive a man crazy. Claiming to be a White Russian, with direct descent from the Russian royal family, this Romanoff Princess had emigrated to Miami from Leningrad two years previously. Quickly finding her feet among the huge Soviet expatriate community, she was put in touch with a man who had 'business' connections, and who sold her a nice new Mercedes with interest rates that weren't going to bust her balls as long as she kept him supplied with information about the wealthy businessmen she now chauffeured in and around the city.

Right now, Ilyana wasn't driving me wild. No, that would come much later that evening. Though she had made me quite nervous by announcing that she had just lost her driving licence for speeding and if she got caught that morning, she would go directly to jail. In spite of this minor impediment, at that precise moment in time, Ilyana was concentrating on driving Daniel directly into the Lion's Den.

It was five a.m., and we were travelling the seventy miles that separates the Marriott Harbour Beach Hotel in Fort Lauderdale with the sleepy Miami suburb of Boca Raton. By a weird twist of fate, I was on my way to the house of one of the most successful paparazzi photographers in Miami, a British expatriate named Chris Bott.

In the briefcase beside me, there was not the kilo of cocaine or hundreds of thousands of dollars that Ilyana suspected I was carrying, but something almost as valuable: the photos from The Spice Girls' video shoot for 'Mama'.

I was on my way to Chris Bott's house to make use of his wire facility to send exclusive shots of The Girls and Their Mums to the *Sun* for the next day's paper.

This cross-country dash had been triggered by the arrival in New York the day before of Matthew Wright, the showbusiness correspondent for the *Mirror*. Depending on your perspective, Wright had turned up in the Big Apple uninvited, to door-step (our word) or congratulate (his word) The Girls and to try and secure a story with photos.

When the news reached me via my side-kick Duff Battye in London that Wright was on a plane on his way over to us, Simon Fuller and I had retired after the Empire State Building shoot to plan our strategic response.

'We can't let these people dictate to us,' said Simon, in between dealing with the calls that were coming in non-stop on the two lines in his plush Four Seasons suite. 'If we give in to them, we're sending out a really bad signal.'

'Well that would make all of Fleet Street think that all they had to do was turn up any time they like and The Girls are just going to roll over for them,' I said.

'Listen, I think you should come to Miami with us, just to be on the safe side,' said Simon. Originally I was to go back to London that night with Chris Heath.

'So, if Matthew Wright turns up, it's a definite NO. I'm not going to let the *Mirror*, or anyone else for that matter, dictate terms to me, or tell me how to go about my business.'

'OK, Simon, I'll change my flight and I'll see you at the airport tomorrow morning. You've got my number at the Peninsula if you need me tonight.'

A little later, I waved goodbye to Chris Heath as his taxi motored into the Manhattan traffic. I felt quite sad watching him leave. I'd come to enjoy his company very much over the three intense weeks we'd spent together.

The following morning, I was at the Four Seasons Hotel at seven a.m. I helped Rachel Pinfold to load all the luggage into a Previa and went to the airport with her to perform an advance check-in for The Girls so that they weren't hassled by paparazzi when they arrived at the airport and could be whisked straight through.

Little did I know that outside the Four Seasons, watching me load up and depart, was Matthew Wright, who, as soon as he saw me drive away, was inside the Four Seasons and on the house phone to Simon Fuller, who answered, imagining it to be his seven-thirty wake-up call.

Wright said to Simon that he wanted a photo of himself with The Girls and a quick interview NOW, before they went to the airport, or he would follow them down to Miami and then on to Los Angeles if he had to. He said he was prepared to persist with his unwanted attentions until he got what he came for.

For the sake of an easy life and despite our unflinching and pontifical stance the day before, Simon caved in and conceded ten minutes to Wright before The Girls got on the bus to the airport.

Which was where I found out about this little bombshell.

Camilla ran breathless from the Previa towards the check-in. 'Muff, have you checked in yet?'

'Err, yeah. Why?'

'Matthew Wright turned up at the hotel and Simon let him

take a picture with The Girls. I've got the film here. Simon said
you're to get it developed, approve a single shot and take it to
Wright at the Paramount Hotel and then take him out to lunch
and schmooze him.'

'What?'

I was flabbergasted.

After all that tub-thumping yesterday and now at the first
sign of a confrontation Simon had caved in and collapsed like a
house of cards.

I felt really angry about this. Once the papers start telling you
to jump, they're on your back all the time, telling the artists to
jump through hoops. You do that once, and they think that
whenever they want something, all they have to do is turn up and
use a bit of coercion and they will get away with murder. They'll
think, well it worked last time, why not do it again? And again.
And again. And again.

I understood that for the sake of an easy life Simon had
performed a swift U-turn, but that didn't make me feel much
better. And The Girls, how did they feel about this?

Three weeks earlier, Wright had made unpleasant comments
about Emma's figure, when he, like some other papers, ran
'those' photos from her Caribbean holiday. Then a week later,
Geri had being pressured by him about her relationship with
Giovanni Laporta. This was followed by the taking of a high
moral stance on Melanie B's confession to *Smash Hits* that she
once stole a pair of knickers from BHS. And now, after all that,
The Girls had had to pose with him for a photo, pretending that
he was one of their best mates. What did they think about that?

When you work for a group in such an intense and intimate
atmosphere, it is impossible not to become emotionally involved.
They become like family. What affects the band, affects you.
When people write nasty things about them, you feel it too. There
is an emotional response, a response that triggers protective

Victoria backstage
at the Brits,
February 1997.

With Diana Ross, backstage at the Brits.

With Elton John, backstage at the Brits.

Backstage at the Brits with Gary Barlow.

Main picture: Onstage at the Brits, February 1997.

**Main picture
and inset (above): With Kathy Acker
at SIR studios, New York,
April 1997.**

Above: At their *Girl Power!* book launch, Virgin Megastore, April 1st 1997.

Leaving the
David Letterman Show,
New York, June 1997.

Right: Baby with Chris Heath at the *Rolling Stone* photo shoot, New York, June 1997.

Right: Victoria at the shoot for the cover of *Rolling Stone* in New York, June 1997.

Main picture: Mel B at a cover shoot for *Pride* magazine. Clockwise, from right: Mel C being shot for a *Melody Maker* cover at The Monarch in Camden Town; Posh at The Ritz in Paris wearing Chanel in the Coco Chanel Suite at a shoot for the cover of *Tatler*; "Are you sure this vinegar is Balsamic, Muff?".

feelings towards Our Girls and feelings of malevolence towards the perpetrators.

So it was not surprising that I was upset. The whole thing left an unpleasant taste in my mouth, but it was a taste I would have to get used to.

The Girls wandered into the airport. They could see that I was angry. Maybe they were angry too, but they didn't show it. Like with everything else that came their way, they were professional to the nth degree and knew that they had to play the game sometimes, even if it meant standing smiling with your arm around someone who had spent the past four weeks making your life difficult. It was all in a day's work. It didn't mean that they liked it.

'Matthew Wright eh . . . the divvy got us, Muff,' said Melanie C, raising her eyebrows stoically. 'So have you gotta go back and give him the picture?'

'Yeah,' I said with a sharp outake of breath.

'Oh make sure you pick a nice one,' said Emma.

'Don't worry, love,' I said, 'I'll make sure you all look nice.'

'And Muff, thanks for sorting out all this Hilfiger stuff,' she added, lovingly stroking her baby-blue puffa.

'That's all right, Emm.'

Geri came up and gave me a kiss.

'Thanks for everything, Muff, are you going to come on to Miami later?'

'Yeah, as soon as I've given this film to Matthew Wright, I'll follow you down this afternoon.'

'I'll see you later then . . .' I knew that, inside, Geri also felt like I did. Maybe she's got a tougher skin than me. Or maybe she's just better than me at hiding her feelings.

I said goodbye to The Girls, climbed into the Previa and asked the driver to take me back to Manhattan. I felt a surge of loneliness and a sense of panic and anxiety. I had checked out of my hotel room, I had to organise a new flight to Miami, go and get this film processed and now make numerous calls to London to let my guv'nors there know what was going on. Oh Mummy.

My meditation practice, which had been fundamental and a great source of support to me thus far, had started to flounder – in part due to having been ill with flu, but also due to jet lag and the mad, mad schedule that never let up. It had left me feeling all over the place. As a consequence, my mental state was suffering: paranoia was running rampant and roughshod over everything, I was feeling totally stressed out and anxious, on top of which I felt physically exhausted and washed out.

I called Simon on the phone from the Previa. He suggested I go to Virgin's office in New York and make that my base for the day. He apologised for the change in plan that morning, but said he didn't have much choice and that I should call Matthew Wright at the Paramount to arrange collection of the film.

I reminded Simon that the *Sun* promised to leave us alone while we were out here and that if the *Mirror* got the scoop, it could cause major problems. Our thoughts had always been that we'd rather be on the wrong side of the *Mirror* than have the *Sun* turn against us, because they have bigger resources.

'What do you suggest then?' he asked.

'If we can stall the *Mirror* by a day, and get something exclusive to the *Sun* then that should be an effective bit of damage limitation.'

'What could we give the *Sun*?'

'Well, they're gagging for the pictures of The Girls and Their Mums. We could give them those as an exclusive.'

'OK. Do that then. I'll leave it to you. And I'll see you in Miami.'

I phoned the *Sun*.

'Fuller's gone and done a deal with the *Mirror*, hasn't he?'

Andy Coulson was on the line, and guess what? He was not 'appy.

'Andy, calm down, mate,' I said as soothingly as I could, given the situation and the six thousand miles of phone cable between us. 'Simon has not done a deal with anyone. Matthew Wright came over here and door-stepped us.'

'So, Simon won't take my calls but he takes Matthew Wright's eh?'

'Andy, Simon doesn't take any calls from the press. You know that. He thought it was his early morning alarm call.'

'Great. So the *Mirror* have got an exclusive of The Girls in America. I'm furious about this. We told you we'd leave you alone and then this happens.'

I told him I could let him have the exclusive on The Girls and Their Mums.

'Well, that's something. Can you wire them to me from New York?'

I explained that the photos were on their way to Miami in Camilla's luggage.

'I'll have to wire them to you when I get to Miami, Andy. Have you got anyone down in Miami?'

'I'll have to try and find someone we can trust. Where are you gonna be in a couple of hours?'

I gave him the number of Virgin's New York office and we agreed to talk later. The driver first dropped me off at Virgin and then drove on to a photo lab somewhere on the Lower East Side, that would deliver the photos to Virgin when they were ready.

On reaching Virgin's uptown offices, I put in a call to Matthew Wright at the Paramount. I got his voicemail. Leaving a message stating that the film was in the lab being processed, I said I would call back in an hour and then concentrated on getting my flight changed.

With me now booked on a four p.m. flight, I called Wright again.

'Matthew, Muff.'

'Muff, hello. Have you got the film?'

'It's down at the lab.'

'Give me the address and I'll go and collect it.'

'I don't really know the address, I gave it to someone here at Virgin and they sent it off for me. Anyway, it's got to be approved.'

'Muff, find out the address of the lab and I promise I'll choose the best shot.'

'I'll have to call you back, Matthew, I'll go and find out the address of the lab.'

I had to stall him. But fate had actually played my hand for me.

The film had already left the lab, but New York dispatch riders being on a par with their equivalents in the UK, they are erractic and difficult to track down. This, coupled with the fact that most of the dispatch riders in New York are cyclists, made its delivery even slower.

I left it as long as I could then I called Matthew back.

'Matthew, it's left the lab and they're trying to locate the dispatch rider.'

'If they can get hold of him, ask them to divert him straight to the Paramount. I have to get that film over to Brooklyn to send it down the wire to the paper.'

'I'll do my best.'

There was actually nothing I could do until the biker turned up so I went to grab some lunch from a deli.

There was a call waiting for me on my arrival back at the office. Guess who?

'Muff, where is that bike? Have you heard from them?'

'Yeah, they've located him and he's on his way to Virgin. I'll call you when he gets here.'

'Don't worry about that. I'm coming straight over.' The line went dead.

Oh hell. It was imperative that Wright didn't get the photo until three p.m. By that time it would be too late for tomorrow's editions. But if he turned up before the bike arrived, or even worse, at the same time as the bike arrived, then there'd be nothing we could do but hand it over.

'Muff . . . It had to be done, mate. I'm sorry, you gave us no choice.'

Matthew had just arrived and greeted me with one of those arms outstretched, shoulder-shrugging gestures that say 'The situation is out of my hands, mate.'

This became even more apparent when Wright told me that New York was the last place he wanted to be at that moment because he would rather be at home with his father, who was dying.

I felt terrible when he told me this. I wouldn't wish that on anyone.

We made small talk for a few minutes and then I left him there, since I had to catch my plane to Miami.

I asked Yon Elvira to choose a good shot when it arrived and left for the airport. It didn't look much like the photos were going to arrive before three p.m. anyway.

Just before I left, Coulson called and gave me the number for Chris Bott, whom he asked me to contact on arrival.

When I arrived at the hotel at Fort Lauderdale, everyone had gone to a dinner with the staff of MTV Latino. I ordered a meal from room service and called Bott.

The one thing that was painfully obvious was that I couldn't tell Bott where we were staying. We were deliberately staying in Fort Lauderdale to fox the paparazzi and press contingent. They would all presume we were staying in South Beach, probably at the Delano. But we were trying to maintain a low profile out there.

'I'll bring my Mac and come over to you,' said Bott, on the phone. 'Where are you staying?'

'Chris, mate, I can't tell you that, I'm sorry. I'm not saying I don't trust you or anything, but I'm not allowed to tell anyone where we are.'

'Are you staying in South Beach?'

'Chris . . . My lips are congealed, mate. I'm saying nothing. Look, I'll come to you if that's OK. Where do you live?'

He gave me his address. He lived out in Boca Raton which, I worked out, was about seventy miles away from where we were staying. Not being familiar with the area, I would have to hire a chauffeur-driven car. And because of the time difference and in order to make Saturday's editions, I would have to leave at five a.m.

I had left messages for Simon, Camilla and Rachel to call me when they got back from dinner.

Simon called first. He agreed it would be disastrous if Chris Bott came to the hotel, and told me to hire a car and driver. I then went to Camilla's room to collect the photo session.

It transpired they had been met by photographers at the airport, but had managed to lose them on the motorway on the way out to Fort Lauderdale. For the moment we were safe, but it was only a matter of time before they discovered our location.

What is their detection method? Well, all The Girls and their PAs were registered under assumed names (as indeed I was), but because Simon needed to do business wherever he went and liked to be contactable, he was always booked in under his own name. So, all the reporters and journalists had to do when they were trying to track The Girls down was call every hotel and ask to speak to Mr Simon Fuller, until that magic moment when the telephonist said: 'Certainly, sir, I'll just put you through.'

Dragging myself wearily out of bed the next morning, I showered and went down to the lobby of the hotel. The concierge directed me to a gleaming black Mercedes with tinted windows. The driver's door opened and a sleek expanse of stockinged leg sidled out seductively, followed by the rest of the body of an extremely attractive young woman, whose modelesque features were crowned by an inordinate mane of brown hair.

She handed me her business card which stated her name, Ilyana Silanovich, and her office and mobile number.

As Terry-Thomas or Leslie Phillips might have said: 'H-e-l-l-o-o-o!'

I took up residence on the white leather back seat and we drove off, past the still and empty beaches fringed by palm trees as the sun began its daily ascent into the cloudless Florida sky.

I don't know if it was my nervous and washed out demeanour or the fact that I kept peering behind me through the back windscreen to see if we were being followed, that gave Ilyana the impression that there was something untoward going on. Just because I'm paranoid doesn't mean *they* weren't out to get me.

She would tell me later that evening that she was convinced she was taking me to a drugs deal. I suppose, this being Miami, it's the sort of thing that happens every day, probably like you or me popping along to the supermarket.

After driving for an hour and a half, during which time she had told me her life story in an accent heavier than lead boots and sexier than I ever believed possible, we pulled into Northeast Seventh Drive and located Bott's plush, sprawling bungalow, replete with pool, where he had lived with his wife and two young daughters since relocating from London two years earlier.

I asked Ilyana to wait in the car. Not so much because I didn't want her to see what was going down (yeah, the rocks were this big, Nastase!), but because I was worried that Chris would ask her where she had picked me up, and then this gorgeous little pussycat would have let our secret out of the bag.

Chris's wife made us a cup of tea and we got down to the nitty-gritty. Chris phoned Paul Buttle, the *Sun*'s picture editor on the freephone number that Chris, as a privileged paparazzo, is privy to. All newspapers have a freephone number for their correspondents and photographers to either phone in their copy, or send their photos down the wire.

Chris chatted with Buttle while I selected the photos and handed them to him to scan into his computer, before sending them down the line.

His other line started ringing. It was one of Bott's paparazzi chums.

'Yeah, he's here now,' he said into the receiver, looking over at me.

'No, he hasn't told me, he says he won't tell me. Really? Oh? You've tried everywhere in South Beach. What about Miami Beach? Hmm, OK. Well, keep trying and let me know if you find out. Yeah, if he changes his mind after I've been so nice to him, I'll give you a bell and let you know.'

He replaced the receiver and came back to the console.

'Well, you'll be pleased to know they haven't found you yet.'

'Ooh that's a relief then, mate,' I said, not kidding at all really.

'But you know we're going to find out where you are, eventually, don't you? You might as well just tell me and save everyone a lot of trouble.'

'Chris, I'd get them cut off if I told you where we're staying. Anyway, there's nothing like the thrill of the chase, is there, mate?'

This was probably one of the most surreal situations I have ever found myself in. I was sitting in the home of a paparazzo and he and all his mates were going mad trying to find out where The Girls were staying so they could make their living that week, and make our lives a misery. How ironic was this?

'You know we're going to catch up with you tonight at the gig. What time are you on stage?'

'Nine o'clock, mate.'

The Girls were set to do a PA that evening at the Hialeah Spring Fair at the Hialeah Race Track on the outskirts of Miami. The gig was sponsored by Miami R'n'B station WPOW 'Power 96' who were one of the first American radio stations to play 'Wannabe' and had been hammering it out since November. The PA was by way of a thank you to the station.

Power 96 had been advertising the gig on air every twenty minutes, so I didn't feel a sense of betrayal by telling Chris the on stage time.

To send four pictures down the wire as 'good for good' takes ages and Chris regaled me with stories of hunting his quarry while we waited.

'I got these pictures of Mike Smith and Sarah Kennedy relaxing round their pool on holiday over here, when they were recovering from their helicopter accident. He was bleedin' furious. He was shouting, "Look, come back and let's talk about it." Not bleedin' likely, I was straight out of there, mate.'

As a freelance, Chris was in touch with all the papers. He'd had the *Mirror* on the phone that morning, wondering if he would cover the gig for them.

'They were very unhappy with that photo from New York, horribly under-exposed it was.'

I explained that it was taken in a rush just before the sun came up.

'Yeah, the picture editor was having a good moan about it. Apparently they were kept waiting all day yesterday for it as well.'

It's at times like this you realise the world is a small place.

'Yeah, the dispatch rider went missing.'

'Oh yeah, a likely story.'

The reason we were only sending four photographs down the line was because the day that Ray Burmiston took the photographs of The Mums with their daughters on set, Jackie Adams had to leave early to go to a dinner dance. Consequently, I had pictures of the four other Girls with their mothers, but not one of Jacqui and Victoria.

This would cause a few ructions the following week. Tony Adams, Victoria's dad, was very upset by this oversight and had words with Victoria about it. And Jackie had a few words with me.

'It's not bloody good enough, Muff,' she said. 'We co-operate with you all the way down the line. You asked us not to talk to the papers, and we haven't. Now you organise something like this and we get left out.'

'Jacqui, I'm really sorry, it was while I was out in the States and it happened off the cuff.'

'Well, you should have rung me. I could have given them a picture of me and Victoria.'

'I know, I'm sorry.'

She was right. I could have phoned, but I was so caught up in the situation in America, I didn't think of it. Once again, I was only human and people do make mistakes. Especially those who are totally exhausted.

The doorbell rang. It was Ilyana. She wanted to use the toilet. As she passed through the front room, she noticed the photos and the computer and I registered a look of disappointment on her face. She returned to the car afterwards and I took her a cup of tea, apologising for the long wait and explaining that it was going to take another hour.

Before we left, the phone rang and once again it was the rest of Bott's press pack, still prowling.

'They still haven't found you,' he relayed, adding as I packed up the photos and closed the briefcase, 'You know I was going to get you followed as you left here. Tag you all the way back to the hotel. But I thought, nah, too much hassle.'

We laughed. And then I thought, oh no, what if that's the old double bluff, what if he has got someone waiting down the road to tail us as we leave? After thanking him and promising to get The Girls' autographs for him that night at the PA for his daughters, I clambered back into the Merc and we took off.

'Listen, Ilyana, there's a strong possibility that we might be followed from here. Could you try and make sure we're not followed, please?'

As she suddenly swerved off the main road and took a few hard turns, I was thrown around the back seat like a cuddly toy round a playpen. Above the roar of the engine she shouted: 'Is OK, in Soviet Union, I was driver for Mafia chief in Leningrad. Plenty time we make pretty car chase.'

After about five minutes, as she slowed down and we regained cruising speed along the motorway, I relaxed.

I explained that I was the press officer for The Spice Girls, a British pop group, and that what I'd been doing all morning was sending their photos to a British newspaper and that photographers might have been following us.

I'm not sure she believed me.

'The Space Girls?'

'No, Spice.'

'I have not heard of them. You have CD?'

'Yeah, back at the hotel, I'll get one for you.'

When we returned to the Harbor Beach Hotel, as I peeled off the $350 our little journey had cost me from my not inconsiderable tour float, Ilyana looked up and said: 'What you do tonight? I know many nice restaurant in Miami. You want go eat?'

'I'd love to,' I replied. I explained I had to go to Hialeah for The Girls' performance first.

'I pick you up here at ten thirty,' she said.

I was feeling hungry already.

The first thing I did was go to my room and call Camilla on her mobile to warn her that the paps were in ardent pursuit and to try and stay away from South Beach. I then contacted Simon to inform him my mission had been successful and that I had made it back to the hotel without bringing any unwanted guests. He suggested we meet for lunch round the pool while he took me through The Girls' diary for the next few months, which he had just finished confirming.

We went through the diary day by day, Simon pointing out any new developments. The first big news was that The Girls had done a sponsorship deal with Pepsi. The Girls were to film a TV ad and feature on a hundred million cans around the world, from the start of the summer. Also there was confirmation that The Girls' next single, the double 'A' side 'Mama/Who Do You Think You Are', scheduled to come out a week before Mother's Day, would feature 'Who Do You Think You Are' as that year's Comic Relief single. Plans were now afoot for The Girls to make a special video featuring Dawn French and Jennifer Saunders.

Simon told me The Girls had been asked to do a promotion for the sports car Maclaren and that, as part of the deal, each of The Girls would receive a brand new Mercedes. The day after that engagement, 14 February – Valentine's Day, he pointed out, The Girls would have to make a nightmare journey to America for twelve hours to appear at a Radio Programmers convention in New Orleans. Mercifully, there would be no press considerations on that trip, so I would be surplus to requirement. What a relief.

Then we had the Brit Awards on 24 February, which I already knew would be one of my busiest days of the year. The other big event in our calendar would be The Girls' first ever live show on the American television programme *Saturday Night Live* in April, where they would be seen by in excess of twenty million people. It was shaping up to be an incredibly busy year.

After a long, solitary walk down to the beach to try and regain some personal space, I went to get ready for Hialeah. The Girls were doing an interview with Y100, a Miami radio station. I listened in while I showered and got ready for the gig. Tonight's show was only a PA with live vocals over a backing track with vocals included. It was never meant to be a live gig.

It was a shame the British press contingent who turned up with Chris Bott never saw it that way. They reviewed it as a live gig and were unsympathetic.

An American football player, Bernie Kosar, who played for the Miami Dolphins had phoned in to the show on Y100 to talk with The Girls.

'Are you the type of soccer star who plays with funny-shaped balls?' asked Geri, while all the other Girls giggled. While he was obviously dumbstruck – there was an awkward silence – Geri gathered pace.

'You sound very sexy, Mike,' Mel B said. 'Do you want to come up to her room tonight? It's room 221.'

Bobby, the DJ, felt the show was running away from him and tried to regain control by asking Kosar about an appearance he made on a US sitcom alongside Little Richard.

Before he got a chance to answer, Melanie B steamed in.

'Hello, Bernie. Why are you phoning up, shouldn't you be off working on your technique somewhere? Your scoring technique? What was Little Richard like? Was he little?'

Kosar laughed nervously. 'He was kinda cool, you know.'

Bobby came in to save Kosar.

'Right, now, we're going to go over to Elaine Turner for a traffic report.

After they'd found out the situation, traffic-wise, in down-

town Miami, the traffic controller asked Posh about her reputation for wearing designer wear.

'It's not what you wear, it's how you wear it,' said Victoria.
'Our philosophy is that you can spend a fortune on designer
clothes and still look awful.' They all erupted into hysterical
laughter.

DJ Bobby was running out of patience and went to a
commercial break. The Girls told me later he took the opportunity to chastise Victoria for swearing on air.

After they came back on air he asked what they thought of
American men.

'The men here are gorgeous,' Emma told him. 'They're so
muscly and these are very good-looking Hispanic guys. You girls
out here are so lucky!'

'What do you think of the good ole US of A, ladies?'

'Well, you know what I think—' began Melanie B.

'Whoah, wait a minute, what's that thing you've got through
your tongue, Scary?' asked Bobby. 'Oh my God, it's green.'

'It's a tongue stud,' explained Scary.

'Didn't it hurt when they put it in?' asked Bobby.

'It was really painful and my tongue swelled right up like a
balloon for days afterwards,' Scary said enthusiastically. 'There
wasn't much blood, though, and I had to drink loads of iced milk
to reduce the swelling. Have you ever thought about using milk
to try and reduce your swelling, Bernie?'

This was all too much for Bobby.

'Well, we'll leave you to think about that f-a-s-c-i-n-a-t-i-n-g
subject while we take another commercial break.'

Later on in the van on the way to Hialeah, Simon ran
through the amended diary with The Girls.

'When are we having some bloody holidays, Simon?' asked
Melanie B, tetchily, with a chorus of yeahs and other sympathetic
noises from the others.

Simon told them that they were going to go to Bali on the 22 April with some Australasian competition winners. He said they had nine days off after that and could either stay on out there, go home or do whatever they wanted to. They chattered excitedly about what they planned to do and how to fox the press about their whereabouts while on holiday.

We drove up to the main gate in the Previa at about eight thirty p.m. and after showing our backstage passes were ushered straight through and escorted to the backstage parking area. Because of a large gang presence and fears of inter-gang violence, everyone else who came on to the site had to go through an airport style metal-detector and were also subject to frisking from the large contingent of police officers present.

The Girls took over the trailer allocated for them and while I prepared their usual selection of soft drinks, they started to run through their vocal warm-up exercises, which culminated in a resounding burst of Girl Power!. The other artists, mainly hip-hop and local latin-freestyle exponents, nudged each other and stared in amazement at these strikingly dressed English girls.

'Who are dose guys?'

An imposing-looking Hispanic guy covered in tattoos came up to me. He was a DJ with one of the other turns.

'The Space Curls? I ain't never heard ad dem, maan.'

As The Girls waited for the act to finish up, I went out front to have a look at the crowd.

It was largely a black and Hispanic crowd. A young, urban, Miami audience. There was a heavy air apparent, with a lot of guys smoking and getting drunk on malt liquor and I found myself thinking, thank God I've got a backstage pass, and I don't have to walk home from here.

When The Girls hit the stage, the crowd didn't know what hit them.

'Hiya everyone! We are The Spice Girls from England and we

hope you're all having a ball, 'cos I know we are!' screamed Geri.

They got into their positions for 'Say You'll be There'. Some of the guys down at the front were pointing lasciviously at the mauve see-through cat suit that Melanie B was wearing. They were obviously excited by the leopard-print bra and knickers peeking through. Geri had bought the cat-suit at Antique Boutique in New York in November, but decided it looked better on Melanie. Geri's hot pants and fishnet tight ensemble was also attracting a lot of male attention.

They kicked into the routine that they'd performed hundreds of times, moving with their usual mix of vigour and sauciness.

The music finished. The crowd just stood there in complete silence. Bemused.

'Whoah man, this ain't hip-hop.'

The Girls looked at each other. They'd had all sorts of reactions to their music over the last year, but never one like this.

Melanie B tried the subtle approach at audience anticipation. 'Hialeah, MAKE SOME NOISE!'

There were a few half-hearted whistles and yells, mainly from the few women in the audience.

'Hello to all the British press out there,' shouted Emma.

'Hello *News of the World*,' shouted Geri.

'I'll tell you what I want, what I really, really want—'

Scary led The Girls into 'Wannabe' and this time there were flickers of recognition among the stoned and beer-flushed faces.

'Ay, maan, ain't dis da one dey play all day on 96?'

I stood at the side of the stage taking photos. Victoria gave me a cheeky grin and one of her classic Posh stares.

The last strains of this multi-million selling pop classic echoed through the air. The Girls were all gathered together at the front of the stage with Sporty down on one knee.

To say the response was lukewarm is something of an under-statement. I think it probably had as much to do with the heavy wafts of exotic smoke that were evident out front and perfumed the warm night air. The audience was stoned out of their heads.

We were straight in the van and out of there.

'That was terrible,' said Melanie B. 'They were all asleep.'

'Stoned, more like,' said Geri.

'Yeah, that was . . . er,' I attempted to describe my response.

'Good,' cut in Emma, 'you were going to say good, weren't you, Muff? You're so polite, aren't you. That was rubbish, Muff.'

'I wasn't going to say good, I was going to say it was . . . interesting,' I countered.

'Blimmin' heck,' added Sporty. 'If that's Americans for yer, you can keep 'em. They were like zombies.'

I fell asleep in the van on the way back to Fort Lauderdale, to be awoken by Simon, Emma, Geri and Melanie B getting out of the Previa to go and eat. Melanie C, Victoria and I headed back to the hotel.

They were on their way to bed.

I had a quick shower and made my way downstairs to meet Ilyana, who was pulling into the car park, spinning her hands behind the wheel, pulling on a cigarette held tightly between her angry crimson lips.

First thing in the morning The Girls were flying on to LA. I was flying back to London late in the afternoon. Which meant I could have a rare lie in. Just as well really.

It looked as though I was going to need it . . .

Chapter Eight

. . . .

ST VALENTINE'S DAY MASS-MEDIA AND THE SAINTLY RELIC . . .

London, 11 February 1997

'*Blimey!* I just don't belive it.'

Geri Halliwell was more than a little surprised. She thought she had just walked straight into a mirror. 'That is just unbelievable. You look fantastic! You look just like me.'

The object of Ginger's stunned outburst was none other than Jennifer Saunders, who at that moment in time could definitely pass for Geri's double.

We were at a theatre in Willesden, the location for the video for 'Who Do You Think You Are', the official Comic Relief single for 1997. The Girls had just arrived to begin their daily toil with hair and make-up and they were thrilled to bits with their reception party.

Jennifer smiled and said 'Thank You', obviously pleased that the three hours she had just spent in make-up and the two weeks she had spent peering through pop mags and studying videos of

The Spice Girls' television appearances had paid off. Her likeness was totally spooky.

Jennifer had put together a group called The Sugar Lumps for this meritorious occasion, pulling in some of her friends from the acting profession in the process.

Dawn French had opted to don the Gucci schmutter to become Posh Spice; Kathy Burke, who plays Waynetta Slob in Harry Enfield's TV show had taken on the gruelling fitness regime that is a prerequisite for anyone seeking to emulate Sporty Spice – 'I am not smoking a fag,' – she told us while demonstrating her new found penchant for deadly drop-kicks and backflips. (The backflips still had a long way to go though.) And Baby's doppelganger was Scottish songstress – Lulu.

Lulu, practising Buddhist and earth-mother, had become just that for the day, a Mum figure exuding much warmth and friendliness to our Famous Five while regaling them with stories from her long and illustrious career. Scary's other half was played by Llewella Gideon from *The Real McCoy*. Melanie B took her off into a corner to explain the finer nuances and advantages of leopard-print versus tiger-stripe. Ten minutes later, Llewella was wandering around intermittently going: 'Aaaaaaaaaaaaaargh!' which was a very good impersonation indeed.

A few weeks earlier at the Comic Relief press launch at Madame Tussaud's, when The Girls had all donned red noses and Comic Relief T-shirts and posed for photos with Jennifer, Dawn and Lenny Henry, Scary had manhandled Lenny and said she wanted him to play her part in the video.

'It's a Girls' thang,' he told her, 'I can't do it.'

Simon Fuller's brother, Kim Fuller, and the man who wrote the script for The Girls' film *Spiceworld – The Movie*, used to be one of the scriptwriters for *The Lenny Henry Show*, and Simon Fuller also A&R'd a Lenny Henry album during his sojourn at Chrysalis Records in the early eighties. Hence the Comic Relief connection.

The theatre was a mad throng of jugglers, tattooed love boys, a wild woman with a snake and other mad carnivalesque people who played the audience in the video.

Three days had been set aside for the video. The first day was for The Sugar Lumps to film their set piece, which would feature at the start, then a day for The Lumps and The Girls to strut their funky thangs together and then a third day just for The Girls, who were actually shooting two different versions of the video – one for Comic Relief with The Sugar Lumps and another Sugar-free version that would feature The Girls on their own.

The day before The Girls were due on set, I had an argument with Rachel Pinfold, one of their PAs.

I was bringing *Top Of The Pops* magazine down to do a cover feature on the band, with photographer Ray Burmiston coming along to shoot the cover and also to shoot photos that I could use for press purposes.

I said that I would be there early and that *Top Of The Pops* would be there at one p.m.

Rachel said that it was too early and that none of us should get there before four p.m. We had a heated exchange. When I was attending a photo session, I felt I had a professional responsibility to be one of the first to arrive and the last to leave, just to make sure that everything was all right and so that I was on hand if anything should crop up and need sorting out.

'We're here to look after The Girls, Muff,' Rachel said, meaning she and Camilla. Even so, with The Girls under siege from the press, I maintained that my presence was required. You never knew what might occur.

Although I didn't realise it at the time, this was the beginning of a change in the dynamics of the relationship between The Girls and those of us who worked at Virgin. It was a change instigated by 19 Management.

Simon Fuller didn't like anyone to get too close to The Girls.

He liked to keep everyone compartmentalised. We were about to become 'the people from the Record Company'. Simon liked to maintain a distance between The Girls and those who worked with them.

His policy of keeping journalists, television people and also the people who chaperone them, i.e., us, in separate hotels when working, as well as ensuring The Girls never over-did it on the work front, enabled him to keep a controllable distance between The Girls and those they worked with.

This situation would develop further over the coming months as The Girls took on more and more outside projects, such as the movie and a glut of adverts and product-placements. Our role would become diminished in the eyes of the management – a situation that became quite upsetting. This would have an impact on the emotional investment that not only I, but other people had made: those who cared about the band and had been working their butts off, while promoting and protecting them for the previous nine months.

It hurt.

When I arrived at the shoot at around four p.m., there was no security on the door and I walked in unchallenged. This was not good. I made a fuss and got someone on the door immediately. However, I was too late.

When I walked in, The Girls were on stage with The Sugar Lumps, performing their first run through.

A couple of hours later, I got a call from the *Sun*. They had just been offered pictures of The Girls and The Sugar Lumps on stage together and they wanted to check the identities of those behind The Sugar Lumps costumes. This was supposed to be a closed set and there was an embargo on anything to do with the video until Comic Relief were ready to do what is known as an 'all around', which means that every paper gets the same thing at the same time.

So, someone had sneaked in earlier, got their photos and had gone off and sold them. Not unsurprisingly, I felt really upset about it, because the management had not allowed me to do my job properly.

It was a madly busy day. In between takes, we were shooting not only for *Top Of The Pops* but for Comic Relief's and our press requirements. The Red Nose was much on display, with The Girls furry red noses being used as competition prizes for *Top Of The Pops*.

The Girls and The Lumps shared a dressing room and bonded quickly, expressing a mutual admiration, with each of The Girls chuffed with her doppelganger.

Baby asked Dawn to speak to her mum, Pauline, on her mobile phone. 'My Mum loves French and Saunders,' she said.

Sporty and Kathy Burke had everyone in stitches while they were having their photos taken together because they discovered a mutual love of Elvis that not only extended to their knowing all the words to songs like 'Teddy Bear', but went as far as both being able to do a perfect Elvis lip curl.

As each take finished they all gathered round a monitor to see how the shot looked and The Girls were staggered by the way the actors had mimicked all their facial expressions, dance moves and gestures down to a T.

As ever, we worked until about one in the morning with the next day's call time for The Girls at eight a.m. I was allowed to arrive at the same time as The Girls the next day, as I was organising another shoot to coincide with their reaching Number One in America, which was expected the next day.

It turned out that after all the hard work and hoo-hah on top of the Empire State Building in New York, the photos were unusable because the helicopter hadn't been allowed to come in close enough and The Girls looked like matchstick men – you could barely make out who they were. So, we planned to shoot

The Girls against a plain backdrop but wrapped in the Stars and Stripes and a Union Jack and then syndicate these to coincide with US chart domination.

When I arrived on set, instead of the usual frenzied activity I found the crew all sitting round drinking cups of coffee. Something was not right.

I spotted Camilla.

'What's going on?' I asked.

'Geri's been taken to hospital,' she said.

'What?' I replied, shocked. 'What's happened? Has there been an accident?'

'Oh don't worry, Muff,' she said. 'She was having a scratch inside one of her ears and a false fingernail got trapped inside. We tried to get it out, and couldn't, so we've sent her along to casualty to see if they can do it.'

Relieved that nothing serious had happened to her, I went along to help Ray set up the flags for the shoot and to chat to Emma and Melanie C who were hanging out in the dressing room with curlers in their hair, waiting for Geri's return before they got changed into their costumes.

There was a contingent of photographers and journalists outside the theatre, including Lee Harpin from the *Daily Star*, but we managed to conceal Geri's accident and journey to hospital from them.

A couple of weeks later, I got a call from Dominic Mohan at the *Sun*, who had found out about Geri's little adventure. Geri, being a sweetheart, had sent the doctor who removed the unwanted cuticle from her ear an autographed photo, which he had put up on the wall in the Accident and Emergency department and one of the porters had phoned the *Sun* to tell them about the incident.

Dominic wanted to do a phone-line and offer the fingernail as a prize. It sounded surreal enough to go ahead with, and he phoned back to check the colour of the false nails she was wearing in the video, so the prize would tally.

The item made the front page and was one of the most memorable, though equally most ridiculous, stories about The Girls.

New Orleans, 14 February 1997

It was two thirty in the morning. Outside the door of the dressing room, armed security men were holding back five hundred extremely drunk radio programmers who were baying for The Spice Girls' flesh. Inside, Mel B was screaming that she felt like a piece of meat. Emma was having a little weep, Melanie C was stretched out asleep under the table and Geri was telling me it was imperative that I obtained a pair of red satin French knickers for her. Now.

Two miles away on New Orleans Bourbon Street, the showbiz editor from the *Sun* and his photograper, who had just flown in from shooting Prince Andrew, were waiting for us, thinking I was about to magic up a shoot involving a heart-shaped bed and five dozen roses. I hadn't seen my flat in a month, I hadn't changed my pants for three days. I'd just flown a sixteen-hour flight to get here, I was going to be working all night; at eight a.m. I was booked on another sixteen-hour flight to work yet another eighteen-hour day on arrival. Why was I doing this? Or more to the point, what had I done to deserve this? How the hell did I end up here?

I am a great believer in the Buddhist law of karma. To put it simplisticly: if you do bad things in your life and hurt other people, bad things will keep happening to you. If you do good things in your life and try not to hurt other people, good stuff will happen to you. God knows, I'd tried my best to lead a Buddhist lifestyle, following a Buddhist code of ethics, meditating regularly and trying to be nice to people.

So what the hell did I do to deserve spending Valentine's Day on a sixteen-hour flight to the States with Andy Coulson as my paramour? I know I'm no angel, but in the karmic scheme of things, I guess I must have done something pretty bad in one of my past lives.

Maybe we deserved each other?

To be fair to Coulson, he looked as depressed as I was at the prospect of spending the next twenty-four hours with me. And if I am to be fair to both of us, it was his fault that we were there at all.

Having known for a while that The Girls had to make this nightmare dash to the States, and also having known that my services would not be required, I had been looking forward to my first weekend off since Christmas. The prospect of two whole days doing nothing but sleeping, eating, reading and a bit of telly seemed like paradise. When you're out on the road the whole time, the simple homely pleasures that we all take for granted become quite important to you.

It was Thursday, 13 February and The Girls had just gone to Number One in America with 'Wannabe'. And by one of those fateful and most convenient of coincidences, despite being arranged months earlier, the next day they were going to travel to New Orleans to be guests of honour at the Gavin Radio Convention. That Thursday, I had a rare day in the office catching up after the two days on the 'Who Do You Think You Are' video shoot.

Coulson was on the line. And guess what? He was *still* not 'appy.

'Listen,' he told me succinctly. 'Either you take us to New Orleans, or we just go out there on our own. It's up to you.'

I took this information down to our Spice Planning Meeting.

The considered opinion was that we take him and I chaperone him for the trip.

'Cheer up, Muff,' Paul Conroy said sympathetically, on seeing that my face was now longer than a piece of string. 'It could be worse, you could be in Accrington Stanley on a wet night checking out some unsigned hopefuls.'

'Yeah, thanks, Paul.' It still didn't make me feel any better. I felt depressed at the prospect of what was to be a completely exhausting weekend.

The day was made busier by Simon Fuller making a snap decision to hold a press conference at Gatwick just before The Girls flew out.

I was in headless chicken mode trying to organise this at the drop of a hat. Then, having made zillions of calls, booked a hotel at Gatwick, alerted the press, booked photographers and organised transport for the teen press, I received a message that Simon had changed his mind and the press conference was to be cancelled. Fine. No problem at all.

As Scary might say: Aaaaaaaaaaaaaaaaaaaargh!@!@**@!

The next morning, I was at Gatwick bright and early. We were to fly via Charlotte, from where we would pick up another flight to New Orleans. Total flying time, sixteen hours.

We were on a different flight to The Girls, the golden rule being that journalists never travel on the same plane as The Girls. Coulson and I must have looked like the Brothers Grimm, so enamoured were we with each other's company.

After we'd checked in, we separated for what was our last hour of personal freedom before we were confined to our seats and each other for one of the longest days of my life.

We were called on board. I saw Coulson on the phone in the departure lounge as I made my way to the gate where American Airlines flight 4648 was boarding.

Having boarded, stowed my Tommy Hilfiger travel-bag in the locker above me and settled into my seat with a bottle of water and a copy of Mixmag, I waited for Coulson to board. The plane was full, the first class section comprising of executive types in suits and me in a T-shirt and jeans. Where was he?

We were all waiting for him now. The stewardess came up to me and asked if I was travelling with him. I answered in the affirmative and said that I saw him on the phone in the departure lounge. They had him paged.

I was starting to worry now.

My paranoid mind said HELLO! and started to race away with me. Where was he? Had he just pulled a number on me? The old let's-get-Muff-on-the-plane-and-then-I'll-just-run-to-the-other-terminal-where-I'm-booked-on-The-Girls'-flight-in-first-class-with-them-and-I-can-have-sixteen-uninterrupted-hours-and-while-I-try-and-get-them-drunk,-pump-them-for-their-secrets-and-innermost-thoughts.

After all, he did threaten to go there on his own, didn't he? Maybe this was his payback for being not 'appy. I could picture him back in the office on Monday laughing about it to his mates in the office . . . 'And then I left him on the plane on his own, while I was with The Girls all the way to the States. Bleedin' beautiful it was . . .'

I was in a flap now. What should I do? Should I leave the plane and try and go after him? Should I stay on the plane and catch up with him in New Orleans? After all, it was not my fault that he'd given me the slip, was it? And if he had, it meant we didn't have to travel together and I could relax instead of being closed-down and guarded for the next sixteen hours. Decisions. Oh decisions.

I had just decided he had stitched me up like a kipper and that at least I could catch up on some of my sleep on the journey when he suddenly made his entrance.

'Andy!'

'Don't look so surprised.'

'I thought you'd changed your mind, mate.'

'Nah, sorry. I was on the phone filing a story for tomorrow.'

'Do you know what I thought?'

'Surprise me.'

'I thought you'd left me here and had done a runner over to The Girls' plane.'

He rolled his eyes heavenwards, exhaled deeply and shaking his head, said: 'Muff, you *really* are the most paranoid person I have ever met in my entire life.'

'Well, it's working with you good gentlemen of the press that's made me like this. Now, what would you like to drink?'

It was a long flight, made bearable by the stewardesses who kept one well fed and watered throughout. I had only one alcholic drink, a large vodka at the beginning of the flight to relax me a little. As a rule, I don't normally drink on long-distance flights, because the effects of jet lag are increased if you drink, but I had another reason not to drink today and that was, I didn't want my tongue to loosen.

On a sixteen-hour flight, one has to make a certain amount of small talk. But that's all it was. Small talk. It was a bit tricky, treading the fine line between politeness and downright lies. As a Buddhist, one of the precepts I try to observe is to speak the truth at all times. As a PR, this isn't always possible or desirable. As a PR travelling on a sixteen-hour flight with one of the most efficient tabloid reporters in the country, it's anything but ideal.

Tabloid reporters are like police officers. They are never off duty. Any information they receive is never wasted, it is stored up for the day it might become relevant. Consequently, each time Coulson gleaned a personal detail from me, I felt like I'd had a wisdom tooth removed.

The flight passed slowly, broken up by two movies and enough food to feed the five thousand. We arrived in Charlotte, lagged and with another three hours' flight ahead of us. As soon as we landed, Coulson went off to the phone to call in and also to find out if the *Mirror* was on its way out there.

At the check-in desk at Gatwick, the clerk had revealed that he'd previously worked for the *Daily Mirror* for twenty years and I'd joked that he was probably phoning in our identities, departure and destination to Matthew Wright. About two minutes after this encounter, we had walked by the resident photographers in the departure hall and they'd nudged each other, recognising Coulson, who shrugged his shoulders and said: 'One of them works for the *Mirror*, you can bet your bottom dollar he'll be on the blower telling them they've seen me flying off to the States.'

So, by the time we'd arrived in Charlotte, he wanted to know if anyone had heard about Matthew Wright making his way to New Orleans. I made a joke about Wright probably being on The Girls' flight on the way out here. Coulson did not laugh.

Because we made a last-minute booking on the flight to New Orleans from Charlotte, all the business class seats had gone and we had to travel economy.

'I bet this takes you back, eh mate,' I joked as we took our seats among a group of rowdy home boys who had been getting drunk in the departure lounge and smoking in the non-smoking area. He was not amused or impressed. It was the first time I'd ever flown first-class. Normally when I took a journalist on a trip we had to travel economy. It was company policy. Once or twice I'd been allowed to travel premium economy, which I thought was pretty swish. But the flight to Charlotte, whoah! When I got back to London, I said to Allie Tyrer, our travel organiser: 'Please don't ever send me back in economy, Allie. Not now that I know what I'm missing.'

A few minutes into the flight, Coulson asked if he could borrow my headphones. He had just bought 'Spicy Talk' an unofficial Spice CD that featured an early interview of theirs. About a year earlier, I had been subject to an ear infection, nicknamed Swimmer's Ear, which had been really painful and I make a point of never lending my headphones to anyone.

I explained this to Andy and apologised for my refusal, but I think he thought I was being funny with him and he seemed even more moody for the rest of the flight.

On our arrival we got a cab to the hotel. Our reservations hadn't come through. I did not have my credit card with me and they refused to let me into my room. For the first time that day Coulson seemed happy.

Guess what? I was decidedly not 'appy.

Coulson took me up to his room, where I left a message for Ray Cooper, who had come over with The Girls. Then Coulson, to his credit, after offering me a beer, got on the phone and demanded to speak to the manager, blasting him for not letting me check in. He told him he was a travel writer for the biggest newspaper in Britain and that, frankly, he was far from impressed. They conceded and let me check in. Sheepishly, I made my way to my room.

We arranged to meet an hour later at nine p.m., in the dining room for dinner. Harry Page, Coulson's photographer had also arrived, having flown in from Martinique, where he had been photographing Prince Andrew.

At the end of dinner, we were all seriously lagging, of the jet variety that is, and we decided to do the shoot and the interview the next morning. Coulson and Page wanted to hit the sack, but I had to make my way over to the Hyatt Regency Hotel, where the Gavin Convention was being held and where The Girls were due to be received as guests of honour.

The Girls were due to arrive at the Hyatt at midnight. They were to be taken to a dressing room to chill out for half and hour before being taken up to the Regency Ballroom where they were to be presented with discs to commemorate their Number One chart position. Then, they were to be led to a sofa, where they would pose for Polaroids with the assembled Radio Programmers, and on to a long table where they were expected to sign autographs for half an hour or so.

I met Ray Cooper on the stairs of the Hyatt, who greeted me warmly and handed me a pass.

'All right, son. How was your flight?'

'Very long, Ray, how was yours?'

'We were held up at Heathrow and we missed our connection at Charlotte, so we had to hire two private jets to bring us all down here.'

'How are The Girls?'

'Tired, but they're troupers.'

'Yeah, I know they are, Ray.'

We made our way past the armed guards who challenged us on the way to the dressing room.

Put your pistol away, mate, I am on the list, and I am coming in.

'Hello, Ravers!' I announced myself with my customary greeting to The Girls.

'Hey! Muff! What are you doing here?' squealed Victoria.

'All right, Muff, what the hell are you doing here?' echoed Melanie C.

A chorus of hellos and similar questions cascaded from the other Girls' lips.

Oh dear. This meant no one had told them I was coming and who I had brought with me. Why did no one tell them? If there was one thing The Girls hated it was surprises. Especially surprise additions to their unbelievably busy schedule.

'I've brought a journalist over to see you,' I said.

'Are you with Peter Lorraine?' Emma asked sweetly.

'Err, no. Actually, it's Andy Coulson.'

Melanie B, visibly annoyed asked, 'Why didn't anyone tell us about this? We weren't told we were doing any press on this trip, were we?' I looked askance at Simon Fuller, who just looked away. This put me in a really awkward situation. Simon had obviously not told them I was coming over with Coulson and they would now blame this lack of a warning on me. I would now look bad because Simon never told them. Because of the increasingly indirect lines of communication that the management enforced, I relied on Simon and the PAs to keep The Girls fully informed.

The Girls were all annoyed. Given the fact that they were all also jet lagged, they were all pretty grouchy.

'So what's he doing here? What does he want?' asked Geri.

'Well, we had to bring him because he said he was going to come over and door-step you otherwise.'

'Yeah, so what does he want to do?'

'Well, it being Valentine's Day, he wants to do something along the lines of lying on a bed with all of you,' I said, adding, 'Well, whatever he wants to do, he wants to do it tomorrow morning. He said he's going to get his photographer to have a scout round early tomorrow morning so he can get some typical New Orleans stuff in shot.'

'No way! We're not doing anything tomorrow, we've got a day off tomorrow, even if it is a travel day. We don't want to have to put any make-up on tomorrow. So phone 'im up and tell him we have to do it tonight,' Melanie B told me forcefully, with echoes of agreement coming from the other tired and angry Girls.

'What time do we finish here?' asked Geri.

'Two thirty,' I answered.

'Well, tell him we'll meet him at three a.m., all right?'

In front of The Girls I quickly conferred with Ray Cooper and Simon Fuller about a possible location. The guy from Virgin America suggested a picturesque bar down on Bourbon Street.

I phoned Coulson and got his voicemail. I left a message apologising and said that The Girls wanted to do the interview and shoot that night and that he was to meet us on Bourbon Street at three a.m. I then phoned Harry Page, as I suspected, not unreasonably, that Coulson was deep in the land of Nod. Page answered his phone.

'Harry, look I'm really sorry about this but The Girls want to do the photos tonight.'

'Andy's already asleep.'

'I know, mate, I've just tried to talk to him, but I only got his voicemail. Could you go and wake him up and tell him I'm really sorry, but it's gotta be done tonight.'

'OK,' Page said wearily. 'You'd better give me the address . . .'

At twelve thirty a.m. we made our way through the service corridors, flanked by off-duty secret servicemen and police officers, and up to the Regency Ballroom, which was packed with a mad throng of screaming, guzzling radio executives whose initial greeting to The Girls resembled the gleeful and unconscious primal screams of excited chimpanzees who have discovered cream cakes are on the menu for their afternoon tea down at the zoo.

The Girls took to the eighteen-inch-high stage, where they were introduced to the crowd and presented with platinum discs to commemorate reaching Number One in America, before posing for photos with the discs and then with staff from Virgin America and the organisers of the Gavin Convention.

The crowd filling the large, smoky room were pressed against the stage, swaying dangerously. They had been drinking heavily all night and some had obviously been at it all day as well. They were rowdy and hooted and hollered as Virgin America's under assistant West Coast promotion man announced they would be moving The Girls over to the special sofa where, they hoped, everyone would be able to take home a souvenir photo.

Just like a day out at the zoo.

The Girls were herded off the stage and through the audience, the crowd opening for a second like the Red Sea and then quickly closing again like a clam that had decided it was never going to make chowder.

After the Girls had endured twenty minutes of slobbered squeezing and pecking, the people from Virgin America discovered someone had stolen a box that contained most of the Polaroid film. Which was just as well really, because The Girls had had enough. They had served way beyond the call of dutiful promotion, putting up with enough insensitive behaviour to last not just this lifetime, but one or two more as well.

They were moved to a long table, where they were expected to sign CD gift-packs of their album for the executives to take home as a memento of the evening.

The Girls were far from happy, but at least they now had a table to serve as a barrier between them and this drunken rabble, each to a man inflicted with the age-old ailment of wandering hands.

I procured drinks for The Girls from one of the many impromptu bars that were located around the room. They all had 'large whatevers'. Whatever gets you through, I suppose.

On the way there, our under assistant West Coast promotions man had made a request that they do a PA tonight, which was last-minute to say the least.

The Girls took to the stage and got in position for 'Wannabe'. They were all holding radio mikes and were doing a live vocal over a backing track which had a vocal on it. The DAT kicked in halfway through the song. Geri shouted out: 'Take it from the top, Mr Selector.'

The same thing happened again. Twice. The third time The Girls just shrugged their shoulders and got on with it in a let's-finish-this-and-get-this-complete-nightmare-over-with gesture.

Ray Cooper and Simon Fuller were both really angry about the whole episode.

We were led back through the service corridors. I had Steve Redmond, the former editor of *Music Week* with me, who wanted five minutes with The Girls for a quick interview. I asked them. It was not the best time.

Melanie B shouted as she made her way with security towards the toilet. 'Haven't we done enough for one day? I FEEL LIKE A PIECE OF MEAT!' Her words echoed down the corridor and the other Girls exchanged sympathetic glances.

'I'm going to be black and blue,' said Victoria. 'They just kept groping me.'

'They were disgusting,' agreed Emma.

'What a bunch of animals,' Geri said, while digging around in her bag for a pair of red satin French knickers that she was going to use in a video message we were shooting to be screened at the *Music Week* awards in a month from now.

Eventually, a wretchedly tired, but super-trooping, Melanie C and Victoria agreed to talk to Steve Redmond for five minutes.

After shooting the video in one take, we prepared to depart for Bourbon Street. As Mardi Gras had finished a couple of days before, I had managed to procure five Mardi Gras masks, which I hoped The Girls would use for the photos. I asked them. Somehow, given what they'd just experienced, I was not expecting too positive a response. I felt guilty asking them to do anything tonight.

'I don't recall seeing these in the new Gucci catalogue, Muff,' said guess who? Yup, Posh.

'Muff, I'm not wearing any mask, OK,' Melanie B said forcefully.

'No way, Muff!' Ginger told me.

'You've got to be kidding,' said Sporty.

I was beginning to get a strange sense of *déjà vu*, already.

'Muff, I'll wear one,' said Emma sweetly, with a resigned things-we-have-to-do-eh look.'

We were led by security out of the back door, therefore thankfully missing the messy remnants of the elite corps of America's broadcasting personnel, and all got into a van to make the ten-minute drive to Bourbon Street.

We pulled up around the corner from the bar. I told The Girls that I'd go and check it out to see if our friends from the *Sun* had arrived. They had. They were both standing at the bar drinking coffee to keep them awake. Coulson gave me a black look, that, unsurprisingly, revealed he was far from happy.

'Andy, The Girls wanted to do it tonight, sorry.'

'This place is no good,' he said. 'It's too dark.'

The bar the guy from Virgin America had suggested resembled a coal cellar during a black out.

'Well, let's just walk down the street and find a brighter one,' I suggested. Three a.m. is early for New Orleans and there were lots of bars still open.

'We can ask one of the owners if we can shoot it on one of the balconies,' I added.

We walked down the road together and found a brightly lit bar, which had the words 'Bourbon Street' illuminated outside in a neon sign. Coulson reluctantly agreed to try some shots there and I asked the owner of the European Jazz Bar next door if we could come in and take some photos with an English group who were in town for the evening.

'Who are they?' the barman asks.

'The Spice Girls, mate, they've just gone to Number One over here.'

'The Spice Curls?'

'Girls, mate, Spice Girls.'

'OK, yeah, sure.'

I walked back to the van, where The Girls were waiting. I started to tell them what we were going to do exactly; that we were going to do the shots outside the bar first and then go into the jazz bar to take some photos and give Coulson a few minutes for an interview.

Ray Cooper and Simon Fuller didn't want The Girls to do an interview, they only wanted them to do the photos. I said we had to give him a few minutes for a chat, at least. I started to explain that for the shot outside The Girls were going to have to keep very still for a minute or so, because it was so dark and Harry Page had to shoot using a long exposure.

Melanie B got up and said impatiently: 'Can we just go and do it—'

'Melanie, can you please WAIT!' I snapped.

'All right, you don't have to bite my head off,' she responded, a little wounded.

'Melanie, look I'm sorry, OK. It's just we've all been up for thirty-six hours now and we're all tired and we all want to go home. But if we're doing this we might as well do it properly, all right? I'm sorry for shouting, OK?'

We drove round as near to the bar as the one way system would allow. The Girls piled off and went over to greet Andy.

'Hi Andy! How are you?'

All showbiz smiles and with as much sincerity as they could muster after having been awake for the last day and a half.

We did the shoot outside the bar, more showbiz smiles, then inside on a small stage posing behind a drum kit and with a mic stand as a prop. After Emma had done her shot with the mask, The Girls then grouped themselves round a table and Coulson asked them how they felt when they heard they were Number One in America.

'We were making the video for Comic Relief when Simon called us. We went mad, jumping up and down and screaming. It was a fantastic moment that none of us will ever forget,' explained Geri. 'Then the director shouted "Action" and we went back to work. I think someone ordered champagne but we were so busy we never got round to drinking it.'

Melanie B told him: 'We are fiercely patriotic. We feel like we're out here doing it for Britain. It's like when Frank Bruno came to America to fight for the heavyweight title, except we're doing a bit better than he did. We want to be successful all over the world and we won't be happy until we are.'

Despite being exhausted, once The Girls started talking they couldn't stop, and after a word from Ray Cooper, I had to go over and intercede, saying: 'Andy, The Girls have got to go to bed, mate.'

It was all smiles and goodbyes and I escorted them back to the van. Once again, I felt very emotional on leaving them and walked with heavy feet back to the bar where the smile had disappeared from Coulson's face. He was in a right mood. Which I thought was unfair. He didn't have to take it out on me. It was his fault we were there in the first place. On Monday morning, his headline would say: SPICE GIRLS INVITE ME TO NEW ORLEANS TO CELEBRATE U.S. TRIUMPH', which wasn't exactly the case. He nagged us to take him there and, because The Girls chose to meet him that night and get it out of the way, he could at least have been reasonable about the circumstances of the situation. He smouldered in the cab on the way back to the hotel.

He had decided to stay in New Orleans for an extra night, which meant I could travel home alone and this time catch up on my much needed sleep. I got to bed at five a.m., and was in the shower at eight a.m., preparing to leave for my flight home when the phone started to ring.

'Muff, Andy.'

'Andy . . .'

'Look, Harry's been out this morning and found a paddle steamer. I want to do some photos there this morning.'

'Andy, they won't do it, mate. Last night was *it*.'

'Look, we don't know if last night's stuff is going to come out. It'll only take half an hour.'

'Andy, they're going to be on their way to the airport shortly.'

'Well ask them to do it on the way to the airport.'

'I can only ask, mate.'

I put the phone down and continued packing. I knew for sure the answer would be a resounding NO. That was why we had done it last night. There was no way they would want to do anything that morning, apart from get on that plane and sleep, baby.

I left it ten minutes and phoned him back.

'I've left a message on their voicemail, mate, but I doubt if they'll call back.'

He erupted, saying he'd been treated appallingly and he was extremely unhappy about it and that the editor was also going to be far from happy. At that moment in time, I was past caring about his complaints and was sick to death of the persistent bullying that had become a feature of my job.

I felt completely numb.

I mouthed some less than half-hearted platitude and went down to get my cab for the airport.

Seventeen hours later, I walked into my flat for the first time in what seemed like months. Before I left to make my way to work, I lit some incense, made an offering to the Buddha as a thank-you for my safe return, drew a hot bath and gave myself a thorough scrub. I wanted to wash away every last vestige of this exhausting weekend in a hell-realm and gargle into obscurity the unpleasant taste I had in my mouth.

A taste I was not getting used to at all.

Chapter Nine

●●●

WOT A PAIR OF BRITS!

London, 24th February 1997

'Charlie, if you're out there, could you please make yourself known?' quipped Mrs Merton as she presented one of the Brit Awards for 1997. 'They're all asking for you backstage. Everywhere you go, it's just charlie, charlie, charlie . . .'

Perhaps they were, but not in dressing room number seven. Forget about cocaine, Our Girls can't even drink Coca-cola now.

The impromptu stack of Pepsi cans; the newly acquired ubiquitous symbol of corporate identity, was piled up on the makeshift buffet in the corner of the room. It might not be the real thing, but knowing that your gorgeous image would soon be scattered round the world with over one hundred million of the little blighters leaping off shelves from Paris to Papua New Guinea must be a very strange feeling. And maybe, just maybe, those lucky kids in far flung places who would be watching the Brit Awards on satellite television, maybe they would end up drinking a Spice can of Pespi at precisely the same moment that one of The Girls was tweaking a ring-pull. What a cosmic thought.

Melanie C told Chris Heath during their *Face* interview that initially she had trouble getting her head round everything that was happening to them. Then she said she realised 'I don't have to get my head round it' and that helped to make everything OK.

If you had actually sat down and tried to get your head round what had happened over the previous nine months, you'd be measured up for your strait-jacket in no time at all.

Take the night of the Brit Awards, for instance. Only a year earlier The Girls were completely unknown and had been at the Brit Awards as guests of the record company, getting pissed, getting even noisier and almost being sick over Lenny Kravitz. Not to mention a tipsy and fronty Geri careering over to Tony Blair's table to famously make him an offer he could not say 'No' to – the opportunity to appear in the video for 'Wannabe'. He declined.

Nominated for five awards back in January and with The Brits looming ever closer, The Girls were both excited and nervous about appearing at this most prestigious of ceremonies.

Having been in attendance purely as guests the year before, The Girls were acutely aware of the fact that their appearance this year served as a benchmark to their meteoric rise.

'We were sat out there a year ago, we hadn't even had a record out, no one knew who the hell we were, and here we are this year opening the show,' said Geri, with a satisfied grin, backstage.

The Brit Awards are the jewel in the crown of the UK music industry. It's the biggest night of the year, the equivalent of the film industry's Academy Awards. It's the night the record industry pats itself on the back and, raising its glass, says: 'Ours is the best industry in the world. Aren't we all brilliant?'

To those sitting out front or sitting at home watching the ceremony on television it must seem like one of the most glamorous occasions in the world. But if you happen to be working there, it's one of the longest days in the year. A day fraught with hectic activity and extreme anxiety.

The Girls arrived at ten thirty a.m. on Sunday morning, the day before the ceremony. Half an hour later, they performed the first walk through of their on-stage routine with Priscilla Samuels, their sassy choreographer. As she led them through a series of saucy catwalk-style moves that would blow the minds of the star-studded audience, The Girls sashayed and preened down the angled stage that jutted out into the mosh pit.

After memorising their moves, they went to change into their revealing and memorable outfits that would titillate the nation when they victoriously appeared on the front pages of all the newspapers on Tuesday morning and on the television that same evening. One camera rehearsal later, and they broke for lunch.

After a light lunch (nothing too stodgy when performing, mind) and now fully made up The Girls filmed the opening sequence that would provide a backdrop as they made their dramatic entrance the following night. They planned on having a very early night. The next day was going to be the best day of their lives. (So far!)

It had been a closed set all day, with no press given any access.

However, the next morning our dear friend, Linda Duff, at the *Daily Star*, would print a story that made it appear that she was in fact at the rehearsals, though she blew it badly when she said she was down at the London Arena. (Doh!)

I arrived at Earl's Court the next day, an hour before The Girls. I was there early to make arrangements for the press photographers, who would be coming to the morning's dress rehearsals, so that they could shoot the rehearsals as though they were the actual performance shots. This was so the pictures would make Tuesday's first editions. Later editions would drop in pictures from the actual show itself.

After depositing my suit in the dressing room, I met Bernard Docherty, the publicist for The Brits, and we went to greet the five lucky photographers who had been granted access to that morning's rehearsal. They were Ray Burmiston, who was shooting for us and Retna – The Girls' picture agency, Dave Hogan from the *Sun*; John Ferguson from the *Mirror*; Richard Young from the *Daily Express* and Dave Bennett for the *Daily Star* and the *Evening Standard*.

We took them to the front of the stage and let them know what what going on that morning. The Girls were due to be on stage at eleven thirty a.m. when they would perform a final run through in full costume and make-up.

The photographers asked if they could use flash. I told them to use whatever they needed. Some artists don't like photographers to use their flash guns because they find it distracting, but it never bothered The Girls. And, like me, The Girls wanted the press to get the best pictures possible. The photographers asked if there were any restrictions on how close to the stage they could go. I told them they could go as close as they liked.

Having marked out their positions for the evening show with gaffa tape, and after signing their Photo Release Forms, the four photographers from the papers went off to have a cup of tea, while Ray and I headed backstage to say good morning to The Girls.

In dressing room number seven, the room was a frantic whirl of activity, with Geri and Melanie C in curlers, Emma sitting in front of the mirror with a gown covering her costume while Lisa, one of the four hair and make-up artists for the day, skilfully applied tender brushstrokes to her pouting lips. Sitting next to her, reading the day's tabloid press, Melanie B was having her exuberant hair stretched and teased into an ever louder shape by Jenni Roberts, The Girls' hair-stylist. The smell of make-up, lacquer, and coffee permeated the morning air, which was also thick with anticipation.

All The Girls were nervous, but they were too busy concentrating on preparing themselves for the rehearsal to let those feelings take over. Their families would be here in the audience tonight which also added to their anxiety.

They had brought three outfits for the day: their onstage clothes, some sumptuous evening gowns for wearing post-performance, when they would be sitting at their table and have to go and collect their awards, and also a change of evening gown to wear at the post-Brits party, which was being thrown for them by Virgin at the trendy Quo Vadis restaurant in Soho.

Having said 'Hello Ravers!', Ray and I made our way back to the front of the stage, where he and the other photographers were setting up and selecting the lenses they would use that morning.

Dave Hogan, the *Sun*'s photographer came up and told me he had heard there was a rogue photographer loose in the building somewhere. Supposedly from the same picture agency who sneaked into the 'Who Do You Think You Are' video shoot.

I started to buzz around like a blue-arsed fly and got security scouring the huge, empty hall for any unauthorised personnel lurking with a camera. I had the sneaking suspicion though, that I was being subjected to a wind up. The photographers knew how touchy we were about unauthorised photos and after a few minutes I got the feeling my earnest machinations were the subject of much mirth from the pit.

There were some children of some of the crew out front getting ready to shoot with their cameras. I felt really guilty when I told them they had to put them away, otherwise they would have the film taken out. Legally, I don't think I had the authority to do this, but I was acting under orders from the management. I did feel guilty about it, especially when I then took out my own camera and started happily snapping away as soon as The Girls hit the stage.

I went backstage to check that everything was almost ready. We received the five minute call. I was on my way back to the photographers at the front of the stage to let them know we were going to roll in a couple of minutes when, to my horror, I saw about twenty other photographers crowded around the sides of the stage, cameras and flash-guns in hand, ready to capture the proceedings on film.

'Oh no! Where did they spring from?' I began screaming: 'OI! NO, NO, NO, NO, NO, NO, NO! WHERE HAVE YOU ALL COME FROM? YOU'RE NOT SUPPOSED TO BE IN HERE! ONLY AUTHORISED PHOTOGRAPHERS WHO HAVE SIGNED THE NECESSARY RELEASE FORMS ARE ALLOWED TO BE TAKING PICTURES HERE THIS MORNING!'

Bernard's assistant, Richard, suddenly appeared and discreetly said in my ear: 'Muff, calm down, they're part of The Spice Girls stage act, they're all from a local stage school. There isn't any film in their cameras, look,' he said, while grabbing one of the Nikons being brandished and opening the back to prove his point.

'Oh I'm sorry, mate. No one told me about it. They weren't here yesterday.'

How do you like your egg on the face? Fried, boiled or scrambled?

Ben Elton, who was presenting the show, introduced The Girls; they all stood at the top of the catwalk with their backs to the arena, Geri's CND symbol standing out. The Girls all reached out and held each other's hands, giving each other a reassuring squeeze. The special effects cannons exploded, the first strains of 'Wannabe' echoed through the auditorium and segued into 'Who Do You Think You Are' as they turned and propelled themselves down the catwalk.

The motor-drives were turning over, the stage crew looked on with amazed eyes and leering smiles on their faces. Even though it was a rehearsal, it left everyone feeling stunned.

As The Girls left the stage and silence returned to the empty arena for a few minutes, the photographers stood around marking up their rolls of film for the bike messengers who were on stand-by. You could tell they got what they needed by the Chesire cat grins that were resplendent on each of their faces.

Ray and I went backstage. Ray was in search of 'Kodak moments', while I had to organise an interview with Louise Gannon, the official reporter for the day who was feeding stories down the wire to all the papers. We had promised her half an hour with The Girls. I went to check when they wanted to do it.

A few minutes later, Louise was surrounded and using her tape-recorder and Biro as a means of defence from the excited onslaught. She asked The Girls about the quote from Liam Gallagher, who had said he wasn't coming to the awards because 'he might chin The Spice Girls'.

Bristling, Scary immediately leaned forward and retorted: 'I'd just like to see him try. I'd quite enjoy getting into a fight with him. Come on, Liam, I dare you. Show us just how tough you are.'

'We prefer Noel anyway,' added Emma. 'He's really nice and he's the talented one.'

It was Mel C who got the cheers later that night when, clutching the silver statue in one hand, she shouted into the microphone: 'Come and have a go, Liam, if you think you're hard enough!'

The badinage between our funky sisters and the Brothers Gallagher would continue for months. At the Capital Radio 'Help A London Child' Awards, Noel Gallagher would get up on stage and cheekily ask, 'The Spice Girls may have cracked America, but when are we going to see them play some live dates?'

'Ooooooooooh blimmin' heck!' squealed Melanie C. 'That cheeky wotsit, I wanna 'ave a word with 'im.' But the cowardly custard who'd been chatting to The Girls just before he went onstage to collect his award, had already scarpered.

Asking how they felt about going to Number One, Geri told Gannon: 'We owe all of our success to Britain and we're proud to be ambassadors of pop for our country.' Later that night she would put her clothes where her mouth was and fly the flag, wearing a controversial Union Jack dress designed by her sister Karen, and featuring a pair of stitched in knickers.

And coinciding so nicely with London Fashion Week, Vivienne Westwood would be proud. Well, actually, she wouldn't, having said on the TV programme *Smillie's People* two weeks previously that The Spice Girls 'were animals with no style'.

In a strange outburst during which the words, pot, kettle and jealous came to mind, she went on to say: 'Their dreadful clothes, their dreadful look. Those Spice Girls have never had any education. They have never been brought up, they have just been allowed to grow up like animals.

'They are just cultivating this attitude that you should push your way to the top, it doesn't matter if you have talent or not.

'What people are marketing is disgusting behaviour as a lifestyle. People should be outraged by it. It's corruption.'

Which was high praise indeed coming from the self-styled Queen of Outrageousness Herself.

'Did the photographers get what they needed at the rehearsal?' asked Victoria after the interview was concluded.

'Oh yeah, they were well happy,' I told her. 'They were all shooting up your skirts.'

'Oh you're kidding,' she said, with a look of exasperation, 'I was still wearing my knickers, I've got some Bikini bottoms I'm going to change into tonight.'

Gradually, all The Girls wandered off, heading home for a short time, while Melanie B went shopping. Geri stayed back in the dressing room and put in an extra hour on her dance routine with Priscilla.

Dressed in her hot pants and heels, Geri faced the full-length mirror in the middle of the dressing room and twisted and turned while Priscilla clicked her fingers to the CD player blaring out from the corner of the room, shouting out the timing and the changes to Geri who responded, never taking her eyes off the increasingly graceful moves that reflected back from the glass.

While Geri made her moves, I camped out in a corner of the dressing room with my diary and mobile phone. We were in the midst of the promotion for 'Who Do You Think You Are', and interview requests and photo shoots had to be accommodated: even on a mad day like this, Spiceworld kept turning.

By the time The Girls returned from the two hour break, and once they had finished getting their hair and make-up done and squeezed into their stage clothes, the backstage celebrity quotient was looking decidely healthy and I collared the famous faces and asked them if they would mind having their photo taken with The Spice Girls.

Elton John walked by. Feeling a little like Dennis Pennis, I introduced myself and asked if we could take a picture of him and The Girls together. He considered my request for a second then gave an abrupt: 'Yeah. OK. What, now?'

I took him to the dressing room to meet The Girls, they shook hands and were quite respectful to him, not covering him in kisses or squeezing his arse. He is showbiz royalty after all.

Rather bizarrely, he said: 'You will go to Number One in America, Girls.' Perhaps he'd been on holiday or something and was a little bit out of touch, because The Girls had been Number One for the past two weeks. Still, The Girls were really polite and showed their gratitude for his encouragement:

'Oh thanks a lot, Elton,' said Geri.

It was all over in two minutes. Elton was on the move again and I went off to hunt down some more celebrities. I spotted Eddie Izzard sitting in the dining area. After introducing myself and saying that I thought he was brilliant on Radio 4's *Just A Minute* with Paul Merton and Derek Nimmo, he responded by saying 'That is very kind of you, I thought I was dreadful on it.' I then told him The Girls were really big fans of his and would he mind if I brought them over to have their photo taken with him?

'Hmmm . . . I'm not sure really,' he replied. 'Err, I'll have to think about that one.'

'I'm being an opportunistic PR,' I said, apologetically.

'Maybe a bit later,' he said. We didn't see him for the rest of the evening.

Before my disappointment could register I spotted Diana Ross hovering in the doorway of her dressing room. She was going to perform a duet with Jay Kay that night, the pair singing 'Upside Down'. I made my way over to her. Her assistant blocked the way with an unfriendly and challenging posture and a facial expression that said BACK OFF! So I shouted past her:

'Miss Ross! Miss Ross! Miss Ross, I'm ever so sorry to disturb you, but I'm The Spice Girls' press officer and they are absolutely massive fans of yours and it would totally make their day if you would be kind enough to let them come over and meet you and have their photo taken with you. Would that be at all possible?'

She nodded her head in agreement and partly to me and partly to her officious assistant said in her rich, soft American accent: 'Sure. I'd love to meet them. I think they're fabulous girls. Bring 'em over.'

I went to tell The Girls. They were all as pleased as punch, particularly Melanie B, who exclaimed: 'Wow! We're going to meet Diana Ross. I can't believe it!'

I led The Girls over to her dressing room.

'Hello!'

'Hiya!'

'How are you?'

'It's great to meet you, Diana, can't wait to see you on stage with Jay Kay.'

She replied regally, but with warmth and affection. 'And I can't wait to see you. Everyone's talking about you in America. Congratulations on going to Number One.'

'Thank you.'

'Thank you.'

'Thank you.'

'Thank you.'

'Thank you.'

'You're very welcome,' said Miss Ross.

'Eyes to me everyone,' shouted Ray Burmiston. 'Thank you, ladies, three, two, one.' Flash. 'Just a couple more please. Three, two, one!' Flash! 'Thank you.'

The pictures in the bag, Clive Black, the managing director of EMI records, who was hanging out with Miss Ross in her dressing room, appeared and The Girls flooded round him.

'Oh, hello, Clive,' said Geri. 'Why did you pass on our demo tape, Clive?'

'Yeah, Clive,' butted in Scary before he had a chance to answer, 'Why did you pass on our tape?'

'I think you all did OK without me, don't you think?' he replied without the faintest hint of embarrassment and obviously amused by this lively exchange. All The Girls started harassing him, as is their party tactic, being both complimentary and taking the Mickey at the same time. In their lively discourse they had all forgotten about the presence of Miss Ross, who slipped back into her dressing room unnoticed and closed the door.

Earlier in the day, I had spotted World Heavyweight Boxing Champion Lennox Lewis sitting at a table in the dining area and told him The Girls were big fans of his and would he mind if they all had their picture taken together?

Charmingly, he said: 'Sure, no problem.'

I went to tell The Girls who were still being made up. Melanie B padded over to him in her bare feet, while Ray and I followed.

'No photos,' she categorically stated. 'I don't want my picture taken at the moment, thank you.' Before shouting: 'H-E-L-L-O! I think you're fantastic!' And promptly sat down in his lap and threw her arms around his neck.

From the look on Lennox's face, he could hardly contain his excitement. Here was one very, very happy man. Vinnie Jones, the Wimbledon football player, who was sharing the table with Lennox looked over, giving him a glance that said: 'You lucky, lucky man!'

Melanie made Lennox flex his muscles and gave them a bloody good squeeze.

In this one small corner of the room we were witnesses to a meeting of sex, strength and beauty incarnate.

A few minutes later Sam Fox, who was presenting an award, came into the room. I asked if she would like to meet Geri. She said she didn't mind. I went to get Geri.

Geri sweetly said hello and, before Sam Fox could reply, was interrupted by an autograph hunter. Sam Fox moved off to one side and then said moodily: 'Are we taking this photo or what?'

I apologised and brought the two of them together. As Geri wandered back to the dressing room, Ray said: 'You'd better not use that shot, 'cause you know what they're gonna put, don't you?

'What?'

'Two ex-page three girls . . .'

'Yeah, you're right, mate.'

Melanie C was more than made up when we grabbed one of her heroes, James Dean Bradfield from the Manic Street Preachers, who were about to win the awards for Best Album and Best Group.

The one person The Girls were dying to meet was Prince. I went to try and arrange it for them, but his security was tight and I reluctantly had to concede defeat.

The Girls accosted one of the New Power Generation who said he would arrange it for them, but it didn't happen.

A couple of weeks later, at the *Top Of The Pops* studio, they would be on the same show together and were gathered outside Prince's dressing room being shouty and still determined to meet him.

'Oh please,' they implored of the enormous gentlemen who were standing guard outside his dressing room. 'Please can we meet 'im?'

'We'll be really quick, won't we, Girls?'

'Yeah.'

'Yeah.'

'Yeah.'

'We will.'

'Yeah.'

The door was suddenly flung open.

The diminutive doyen of planet cool stood there demurely.

'Let them in,' he said to his bodyguards.

'Oh T-H-A-N-K Y-O-U!' shouted Melanie B, as they were ushered into his inner sanctum.

'What do we call you?' asked Melanie B.

'Squiggle?' asked Emma, doing her best not to giggle nervously.

'You can call me, Friend,' said Prince.

After the motor-driven, air-kissed whirl, The Girls retired to their dressing room and threw everyone else out. They wanted to be on their own for half an hour before they went on stage. To do their vocal exercise warm ups, to compose themselves, to concentrate on the task ahead of them, to group together and to give each other strength and focus.

While The Girls were locked away in their dressing room, I suddenly did a double take and thought I was going mad. The Girls had just walked into the backstage area and were walking up to the dressing room; but they were already inside the dressing room. I could hear them.

It transpired that these arrivistes were in fact one of the growing number of tribute bands, namely, Nice 'n' Spicey, who had just pulled off a great stunt. Turning up at the front door in a white stretch limo, they had been ushered, waving and blowing kisses, through the screaming crowd and right to the door of the dressing room by security who thought they were the famous five.

The buck stopped there though. They asked if they could meet The Girls. They couldn't have picked a more inappropriate moment.

'Get them away from here,' snapped Nikki Chapman, 'I want them out of here, now!'

As the minutes to showtime ticked by, the tension was building. I tried to turn my tension into action as I asked security to move an Italian television crew who had been camped right outside The Girls' dressing room for the past hour, refusing to move and filming when we asked them not to. They were finally told by the Brit Organisers that if they did not move away from the vicinity of The Girls' dressing room, they would be thrown out.

My mobile phone was ringing. It was Andy Coulson. He wanted to know if it would be possible to either come backstage and have his photo taken with The Girls or to go to their table and do it there. I said that backstage it was chaos and there was no way, but out at the tables later, it might be possible.

All of a sudden it was time to go. The Girls were taken through to their positions at the back of the stage, ready to climb up on to the catwalk. A last-minute hug for each other and they were primed ready. Five coiled springs ready to release their pent-up energy – the moment they'd spent weeks rehearsing for and waited their whole lives for was here at last.

Five girls who will always remember this as one of *the* nights of their lives.

Shouting 'Good Luck!' I ran round to the front of the stage. The mosh pit was packed with a fevered crowd, hot and sweaty with anticipation.

The lights went down and a huge cheer greeted Ben Elton as he approached the dais. 'Ladies and Gentlemen, Margaret Thatcher was due to appear with The Spice Girls, but unfortunately her belly-button ring has gone septic. Please put your hands together and welcome: Posh, Sporty, Ginger, Scary and Baby.......T-H-E S-P-I-C-E G-I-R-LS!!!'

The cannons exploded and the lights revealed Our Girls standing with their backs to us as the first few bars of 'Wannabe' thundered round the packed arena. Whistles and cheers ringing in their ears, The Girls turned and strutted their funky way into 'Who Do You Think You Are'.

In what seemed like seconds, it was all over and we were backstage again escorting The Girls back to the dressing room so they could get changed quicky and go out to their table.

As they came out of the dressing room for the second time half an hour later, people gasped, their jaws dropping as The Girls were led by our team of security out to their table in front of the stage.

Geri was wearing a very low-cut red-sequinned dress that was half Jessica Rabbitt and half Dolly Parton. Victoria was wearing a diaphanous evening dress, which almost revealed what she had had for dinner, while Melanie C, looked decidedly unsporty in a long brown skirt that swept the floor behind her.

The light reflected off Emma's silver-spangled number, while

Melanie B's tiger-striped trouser suit with matching bra was stylish, while still being distinctively Scary.

Twice The Girls were called from their table and, led by Jerry Judge, made their triumphant way up to the stage. First for winning the award for Best Single for 'Wannabe'; a little later grabbing the gong for Best Video for 'Say You'll Be There'.

After being presented with the award by Frank Skinner, who quipped, 'I wish they were coming home, coming home . . .,' the jubilant Girls gushed their thanks and Geri caused a roar of consternation from the crowd when, excitedly thrusting the trophy high above her head, one of her breasts popped out of her dress for a second.

Nikki Chapman spoke to the production crew to make sure that this up-front performance was edited from the television highlights.

Sheryl Crow, in her acceptance speech, took the stage and said: 'I'd like to thank The Spice Girls for not being in my category.' The vibe outfront and backstage was incredible, there was a tangible feeling of the moment belonging to The Girls and it was magic.

As they came off stage, we led them to the press room, which was like a long corridor with about two hundred journalists, photographers and television crews down one side behind some barriers.

I wanted Ray to take some shots of The Girls holding their awards, which, after an artist has taken acceptance of them onstage, have to be given back before they return to their table. The awards are then engraved and sent to the artists about a month later. I asked if I could borrow two awards for photo purposes. We got The Girls to pose with phones and the awards, as though they were on the phone to their families. After some shots in front of the Britannia Music backdrop, a security guard retrieved these prized objects from The Girls' grasp, and we all made for the dressing room.

The Girls were getting changed into their third outfit for the night and while they waited for their cars, they sat around exchanging chit-chat about whom they had spotted out front and who was coming to their aftershow party.

There was a knock at the door. It was Melanie B's mum and dad. Melanie introduced Martin, her dad, to me. He looked so proud. As did her mum, Andrea.

After The Girls had gone, I stayed behind waiting for the bike messenger to take Ray Burmiston's photos to the lab. Arriving at Quo Vadis about an hour later, there was a real scrum at the door. This was the hottest ticket in town that night and everyone wanted to be there.

Including the tabloids. Who, once again, were not invited. I had a quick chat with Lucy Rock from the *Mirror*, who was on door-step duty. I proffered apologies that I could not get her in and made my way upstairs.

The place was packed solid with a lot of very drunk people. Having worked all day, by this point not a drop of alcohol had passed my lips; but I had time for a drink before I had to go to the photo lab at three a.m. to approve the shots for the next day's papers.

Pushing my way through to the bar, I spotted Andy Coulson. Oh dear. How did he get in? He was not supposed to be here. I had a brief chat with him.

'Andy, you'll be the death of me,' I said jokingly. 'You're not supposed to be here, mate.'

'Well I'm a friend of the people who do the PR for Quo Vadis, but I saw Ray Cooper at the show and he said it was all right.'

'Oh did he?' I relaxed, 'Well, that's OK then. I hope you have a nice time. I'm gagging for a drink, I'm off to the bar. See you later.'

However, while at the bar, having secured a large vodka and tonic, I was told by someone that The Girls didn't feel comfortable having anyone from the tabloid press at the party because they couldn't relax and let their hair down and I was told to ask Andy to leave.

A strange feeling of *déjà vu* came over me.

This was starting to turn into a habit. This time I downed the vodka first.

I went back over to Andy.

'Andy, look, I'm sorry but I've been requested to ask you to leave, mate.'

'But Ray Cooper said it was all right.'

'I know, mate, but there's been a bit of a mix-up. I'm really sorry. It's just that there aren't supposed to be any tabloid reporters here, and The Girls feel they can't relax while there are.'

'I don't believe this. What do we have to do to prove it to you? We're their friends. We love The Spice Girls. What do they think I'm gonna do?'

Over the coming year Andy Coulson would indeed display a loyalty that prevailed during the media backlash that shook Spiceworld after the sacking of their manager, Simon Fuller.

'I know, mate,' I replied apologetically, 'but I'm sorry, there's nothing I can do.'

He put his drink down, turned on his heel and angrily stomped out. His farewell ringing in my ears.

'OK, but I'm telling you, I've been thrown out of better parties than this.'

Oh dear. I was gonna be dead meat. As Oscar Wilde might have said: 'To throw the *Sun* out of one party is unfortunate, but to throw them out of two parties is pure recklessness.'

A week later, The Spice Girls made the record books yet again. With the release of 'Mama'/'Who Do You Think You Are?', they became the first band ever to go to Number One with their first four singles. In the process, they also made a record amount of money for Comic Relief, who declared it to be their most successful appeal so far.

That same week was also a landmark for me, when I collected a trophy from Jonathon Ross, host of the 1997 *Music Week* Awards, who charmingly declared as he did the honours: 'It must be really hard trying to write all those press releases with one hand, Muff,' after a panel of eight media professionals decided I'd earned the 1997 PR Award for my Spice Girls' campaign. I felt tremendously honoured. It was a wonderful affirmation, and for my efforts to be acknowledged in this way was the icing on the crazy cake we'd spent the last nine months baking.

A cake that was about to be adorned with the proverbial cherry, when The Spice Girls were asked to perform at a gala evening to mark the twenty-first anniversary of the Prince's Trust and we learnt that Prince Charles had personally requested The Girls' presence with a handwritten letter and wished to have *his* photo taken with *them*!

If only he knew what he was letting himself in for . . .

Chapter Ten

· ·

NICE PLANET . . . WE'LL TAKE IT!

Fax
To: Muff Fitzgerald
  PR of The Year, Virgin Records
From: Linda Duff
  Rave Column, *Daily Star*
Date: 22nd April 1997

Dear Muff

I hope you're feeling better after your recent illness. After my recent trip to New York I'm glad to say I'm feeling much better too!

But I just thought I'd clear up in writing a couple of points.

We didn't mind too much being chucked out of the hotel by the FBI heavies. But I just felt it would have been a little less frightening if somebody from your camp, yourself or an assistant from the management, had simply phoned us and asked us to go. We thought we could keep a respectful distance from the group while still covering the event, but that obviously wasn't working out, for all parties.

What I do mean to make clear is that on absolutely no account would Nick have taken any picture of The Girls without their permission. A couple of incidents were unfortunate. Geri and Mel B met Nick in the lift on our first day and jumped out in horror. He did have a camera around his shoulder which he did not, and would not, on my orders and under any circumstances, attempt to use.

Then again, in the gym: while Nick was truthfully making an enquiry at the hotel, he was actually accompanied into the fitness centre by a member of the security staff who was showing him around!

He was not stalking them or attempting to get a paparazzi pic.

Bad luck number three: after that incident he went to get two coffees and on his return again met Geri at the lift!

He had his camera with him on these occassions simply because if The Girls had said yes to any picture, he would not be forced to miss the opportunity by not having his gear on him.

Furthermore, how could anyone take a pic with two steaming cups of coffee in his hands?

We're sorry to have upset them but we really didn't mean to.

Thankfully, the Chinese torture inflicted by the FBI bullies – who'd been convinced into believing we were from the gross American supermarket Star – is healing up and the company is paying for our skin grafts to cover our scars!

Lotsa luv Muff.

See ya,

Linda Duff

'I think I might get a new piercing while I'm here in New York,' announced Melanie B, in one of her Scarier moments. 'I bet that would give my boyfriend a shock when I get home, wouldn't it?'

It was going to be one of those months.

A mad month that saw their album *Spice* follow 'Wannabe' to the top of the US charts, The Girls played their first ever live performance viewed by over twenty million Americans, swiftly followed by a memorable meeting with Prince Charles when they were His special guests at a Gala Evening for the Prince's Trust charity.

And not even the defence or deference traditionally accorded to the heir to the British throne would save His Royal Highness, the Prince of Wales, from a conversation with The Girls that included detailed reference to piercing and his great-great-great grandfather, Prince Albert.

The Spice Girls may have been lamenting their ever diminishing personal freedoms, the inevitable loss of liberty that hangs off the coat-tail of celebrity like a gatecrasher at a party, but the bonus was that their social circle was expanding at an equally monumental rate.

Within a week of cementing their Royal Connection with a typically irreverent but affectionate lipstick assault, combined with a grandly extravagant goosing of the regal buttocks – a gross insolence which might have had them all beheaded only a few hundred years ago – The Girls discovered they'd made a connection of another kind. Victoria found herself named in a trial at Woolwich Crown Court, which involved £39 million worth of cocaine, having unwittingly shared a drink with undercover regional crime squad officers on the job in more ways than one, and who were on the trail of a certain Charlie Kray.

The only thing pierced on this occasion was Kray's defence and he was sentenced to serve twelve years in prison.

These delightful associations were to come later. Right now, the air was once again delicately scented with powder and perfume, The Girls were sitting on chairs watching their reflections in a large mirror, while $1,000-a-day hair and make-up artists meticulously groomed and preened. Our fab five were relaxed and ready to catch up on the New York gossip.

'Why is it nearly all the men who work with us are gay?' a frustrated Melanie B demanded during this break in rehearsals for the American TV show, *Saturday Night Live*.

They were having their hair and make-up attended to in a small rehearsal room at SIR studios, a few blocks up from Time Square. Next door, the main rehearsal room was the size of a cathedral, filled at one end with the monitors, drums, keyboards and bank of amplifiers that were the property of the *Saturday Night Live* house band. The Girls were here for a week, rehearsing with the band and Kenny, their new vocal coach, in this air-conditioned sanctuary just seconds away from the hot, humid and sometimes dangerous streets of New York City.

The mood was light, Melanie B enthusiastically discussing the pros and cons of piercing with Kathy Acker, the gifted American writer who sadly died from cancer in December 1997. Impressively tattooed, Kathy also had her fair share of piercings, and they swapped tips and advice.

Throughout their exchange, Emma looked increasingly pale and uncomfortable, especially when the discussion turned to infections and discharge.

'Oh please,' she exclaimed, 'can we change the subject? The thought of someone doing that . . . This conversation is making me feel ill.'

Tattoos were naturally the next things to be compared and discussed. Kathy had a beautiful back piece, which coincidentally was done by the same guy in London who did my tattoo.

Melanie B told Kathy that the Japanese symbols near her

belly button meant: 'Spirit, heart and mind, because that's what fuels me; communication fuels me. You learn about yourself, about other people and life in general, through communication.'

However, as we were finding out, in Spiceworld, the pathways of communication did not always run smooth. The Girls concluded their two-hour interview with Kathy and we departed, leaving them in the reassuringly safe hands of Detectives Capelli and O'Sullivan, who were providing first-class protection duties. I flew back to London and went straight to work on arrival, red-eyed and bleary with jet lag.

Early afternoon, the next day, the phone rang. It was Linda Duff.

'Muff!' she said with surprise. 'What are you doing there, I thought you were supposed to be in New York?'

'I was, Linda, but I just got back this morning.'

'Oh no, we probably passed over the Atlantic somewhere. We've just arrived. Oh no, that's a real shame, we've come over to cover the *Saturday Night Live* thing and I thought maybe you could sort something out for us.'

'Linda, I'm sorry, but they're not doing any press.'

'Oh well, we'll just stick around and see what happens.'

Linda and her husband, the photographer Nick Tannesley, were staying at the Four Seasons, the same hotel as The Girls. I knew this would make The Girls uncomfortable, they would feel besieged.

Through my office windows, which looked out over West London, the drab sky was as grey as a pallbearer's face. I sensed a storm was on its way.

First thing the next morning the phone rang.

It was Linda Duff.

'Muff, thank God! Muff, can you do something to calm things down here? Geri thought Nick was following her around the hotel and now there's two FBI men at the door saying we have to pack our bags and leave. Can you phone The Girls or someone from their management and explain for us?'

'I'll call them for you, Linda, but there's not really too much I can do. The situation is out of my control really.'

As politicians, millionaires and movie stars choose to reside at the Four Seasons, security is extremely tight and the hotel management take a dim view of the infringement of any guest's privacy. Which is precisely why The Spice Girls always choose to make it their base whenever they're in New York.

It might be summer outside, but as Linda and Nick loaded their bags into a yellow cab a short time later, they were in the winter of their discontent.

When Saturday came, The Girls were introduced on the show by Rob Lowe, and performed 'Wannabe' and 'Say You'll Be There' to a warm reception from the studio audience and a mixed reaction from the critics.

The Girls were gutted that they had to turn down an offer to go to dinner with Robert De Niro, who was also a guest on the show, because they had to leave at dawn to fly out to Taiwan for further promotion.

From Taiwan, the never-ending promo trail led to South Korea for three days and from there to the beautiful island of Bali, where The Girls entertained a hundred Australasian competition winners for a day, and caused a bit of controversy when they attempted a Maori dance ritual that is only supposed to be performed by men.

Two paparazzi were thrown into jail, when after being thwarted in their attempts to take pictures, they intimidated and then stole the photos from two ten-year-olds who had just collected their souvenir snaps from a local shop.

After a well earned nine-day respite, The Girls regrouped in England in order to rehearse the three songs they were to perform live with an orchestra for the Prince's Trust gig.

The Spice Girls were first linked to the Royal Family back in November when the *Sun* printed a story with the headline 'WHAT WILLS ROYALLY ROYALLY WANTS!', which claimed that Prince William had replaced a poster of *Baywatch* star Pamela Anderson in his room at Eton, with a poster of Baby Spice.

When they heard this news, The Girls were thrilled. Particularly Victoria, a huge fan of Princess Diana, who secretly hoped that 'We might all get invited round to Kensington Palace for tea!'

Princess Diana was something of a role model for Victoria, and she was deeply upset by Diana's tragic death, as were all The Girls.

The appalling circumstances of her demise carried a particular resonance for The Girls, who, like Princess Diana, had to face the paparazzi on a daily basis and were themselves subjected to frightening high-speed chases on more than one occasion.

The paparazzi attentions had also intensified for Victoria around this time because she had just started going out with David Beckham and the couple were hotly pursued wherever they went.

David, of course, would be in the audience that night.

A short time before they were due to meet HRH before the show, an aide from the Palace came to their dressing room at the Manchester Opera House to brief them on royal etiquette. He said that on no account were they to touch the Prince.

Big mistake.

Telling The Girls that they aren't allowed to do something always makes them do the opposite. They see it as a challenge, something one of The Girls will dare another to do.

As the Prince was introduced to them, Melanie B leaned across and landed a loud kiss on his face, cheekily asking 'Can we come to dinner, please?'

Geri, in a revealing trapeze artist's outfit, then made the lipstick ring stereo, declaring, as she brought her laughing gear to One's esteemed cheek: 'I think you are really sexy.'

And then Ginger sealed the moment by swiftly grabbing the Royal Posterior and giving it a good squeeze.

Hello brown eye, indeed.

The historic shot of The Girls with the Prince would make all the front pages, and The Girls agreed that it was the best night of their lives . . . (So far!)

A week later, and The Girls were in the headlines again, this time linked to another Charlie.

Mrs Merton had a point after all.

It was indeed turning out to be Charlie, Charlie, Charlie.

One of the most bizarre coincidences occurred the night that Victoria's old boyfriend, florist Stuart Bilton, whom she left for David Beckham, took her for a drink at the Swallow Hotel, in Waltham Abbey, Essex.

While there, they were approached by two 'businessmen', who bought round after round of drinks.

'I thought there was something a bit odd about them at the time,' said Victoria.

They were in fact undercover police officers, acting as part of an investigation into Charlie Kray, who had allegedly offered to supply £39 million pounds' worth of cocaine. The two officers were at the Swallow Hotel waiting to receive an initial consignment of five kilograms of cocaine.

While they were waiting for the drugs to be delivered, they spotted Victoria and Stuart at the bar, the men introduced themselves and bought drinks.

In court, giving his evidence behind a screen, to preserve his anonymity, one of the officers known as 'Jack', said it was a night he would never forget.

It would be a month both The Girls and the public would

never forget either, as Spice Girls entered the record books yet again, when they became the first British act to go Number One in America with their debut album, as I repeated a thousand times over the phone.

Emma would remember May as the month her ex-boyfriend Mark Verghese, whom she'd finished with some weeks earlier, sold his story to the *Mirror* for £20,000.

The last of the old boyfriends went when Melanie B ended her three year relationship with engraver Richard Meyer, and she was soon snapped by the paparazzi out on the town with the new man in her life, Icelandic businessman, Fjolnir Thorgeirsson.

After the Princes's Trust show, The Girls were due to fly out to America to appear on the *David Letterman Show*. It was around this time that the lines of communication with 19 Management became increasingly difficult.

We were now at the end of our cycle of releases. We had finished working the four singles from the album *Spice*, which was still selling exceptionally well. The attitude that emanated from the management offices was that our pivotal role in promotion, protection and suggestion was no longer vital – The Girls were going off to work on their film for three months, before they started work on their second album, which was to be released in November 1997.

Up until the end of April, each department at Virgin was issued with a copy of The Girls' diary, which enabled us to plan and work in tandem with the management company. At the beginning of May, we were told the 19 office was no longer going to be giving us The Girls' diary. Consequently, we didn't have a clue what they were doing. Which, frankly, was not just embarrassing, it was totally impractical.

Trying to organise anything to do with The Girls became an excruciatingly painful process.

While the American press had been cynical at first, deeming

The Spice Girls nothing more than a 'manufactured' pop group, after they had been Number One with 'Wannabe' for four weeks and then their album hit Number One, they could no longer be ignored.

They weren't. *Rolling Stone* offered them their cover. Yet another accomplishment – something even Oasis hadn't pulled off. (They had been offered the cover but had blown it when Liam walked out of the photo session.)

Chris Heath was commissioned to write the feature and although the press office in America was making arrangements for this, I became involved in trying to sort out as much access as possible for him.

The management company wanted to keep access to a minimum. They said that as Heath had written *The Face* cover feature, he would need less time to write the *Rolling Stone* story. *Rolling Stone* said if that was the case they would send another journalist – whoever was to write the story needed enough time to write an in-depth feature.

Once again, I was trying to mediate between the two sides. I flew out to New York for the *David Letterman Show*.

The Girls had flown in straight from a triumphant appearance at the Cannes film festival, where they appeared on the roof of the Hotel Martinez and made journalists perform a 'Mexican wave' and were deemed to have stolen the show as they touted business for their film, *Spiceworld – The Movie*.

I found Camilla Howarth outside the building, where hundreds of ticket holders were queuing in the middle of a scorching Manhattan afternoon to see the show, which is pre-recorded at five p.m. as 'live' and goes out later that evening.

She told me The Girls were in their dressing room downstairs. I wandered down and found them all together talking to Simon Fuller.

The atmosphere seemed tense. The Girls were distant, almost

unfriendly. I put it down to the fact that they were nervous about appearing live on coast-to-coast television.

I greeted The Girls and Simon, and distributed five copies of the latest issue of *Top Of The Pops* magazine. They were on the cover. A couple of muted thank yous and I left the dressing room and went upstairs to organise a quick photo outside with Andy Coulson, who had also come over for the *Letterman Show*.

We agreed to do a quick shot as soon as they had finished their camera rehearsal with Andy and The Girls lined up alongside a yellow cab outside the backstage door. There was a problem, when Alan, one of The Girls' security men, recognised the photographer as the woman who had taken photos of The Girls while they were asleep on a flight from Canada to New York, back in January.

'The Girls won't let her take the picture,' he told me.

Luckily, Liz Simon a photographer from *TV Hits*, who was there with editor Ian Mcleish, was on hand and agreed to take the photo instead.

I went back inside the studio where The Girls were performing a run through. All of them were wearing puffa jackets or sweatshirts as the temperature in the studio was freezing – David Letterman prefers to keep the atmosphere cool, so that he and his guests stay sharp, and do not feel drowsy under the studio lights.

The Girls were performing 'Say You'll Be There', which had entered the Billboard Top 100 at Number five, the highest ever entry for any UK single in the thirty-nine year history of the chart, beating The Beatles who had entered at Number Six in 1970 with 'Let It Be', a feat they repeated in 1995 with 'Free As A Bird'.

Backstage was a whirl of activity, with the musicians making last-minute checks on their equipment while The Girls had a last-minute run through their scales with their vocal coach in the dressing room downstairs.

I was standing in the corridor that leads to the studio when a cry came down the stairs that seemed to be taken as a mantra by everyone around me. 'DAVID'S COMING! DAVID'S COMING!'

With that I was suddenly and rudely turned and told to face the wall while he passed. Apparently, this is part of his ritual as he goes onstage, no one is allowed to look at him.

Introducing The Girls, Letterman announced that their album had just gone to Number One, saying: 'There's Scary Spice who is hip-hop Spice, Sporty Spice your soccer fanatic, Posh Spice who is the group's fashion and style guru and Sexy Spice who is a former nude model and lap dancer, and Old Spice who loves aftershave—'

As they brought the show to a close he was subjected to a Spice lipstick attack and looked uncomfortabe as Victoria ruffled his exquisitely coiffeured hair.

Straight after the show, The Girls were mobbed as they got into their Previa, waving to the waiting fans before they were swallowed-up by the blacked out windows and sped off to an engagement with America On Line, where for an hour, they talked to surfers all over the world.

Asked by a fan what type of a man she was looking for, Geri typed into her console: 'OK, I'm looking for the brain of Einstein, the body of Arnie, the wit of Robin Williams and the style of Rudolph Valentino.'

Melanie B's terminal broke down and after she was taken to a console in another room, she announced, 'I want one of these. Can I have an Internet?' She was asked by a fan what her favourite sport was. 'Bedroom activities,' was her reply.

The next day was the photo session for the *Rolling Stone* cover, which was being shot at photographer Mark Seliger's plush studio, overlooking the Hudson River.

The Girls were going to do two looks for the shoot – all clad in in vampy black for the cover, followed by a college look which would be shot as inside a football locker room for the insert.

The Spice Girls were obviously a big deal as Jann Wenner, the publisher of *Rolling Stone*, turned up with his children who demanded autographs.

The Girls sealed their trip with an appearance on *Live with Regis and Kathy Lee* and then on the *Rosie O'Donnell Show*, and they still managed to find time to do a book signing, autographing copies of their book *Girl Power!*

The Girls had also signed books in London on 1 April, at the Virgin Megastore, two days after their much publicised launch of Channel 5.

Five hundred competition winners who had received their tickets through Capital Radio were taken by coach into the Megastore, where they queued up to get their books and other merchandise signed by The Girls.

Such was the whirlwind speed with which this event had been organised that The Girls hadn't had a chance to see their own book before they came down to meet the public. On arrival at the signing area, they took a few minutes in front of the world's press to have a quick read.

The day after the signing, the press office at Virgin Records had about two hundred angry and distraught callers on the line. The Girls had signed the vinyl front covers of Girl Power! with felt tip pens, so that by the time the lucky fans had reached home with their newly acquired treasured autographs, most of them had rubbed off!

May ended just as gloriously as it had begun for The Spice Girls when they won two trophies at the prestigious Ivor Novello Awards, taking home the award for International Hit of The Year and the award for Best-Selling British Single for 'Wannabe'.

It was also Melanie B's twenty-second birthday and as they went onstage to collect the award, Geri asked the five hundred strong audience to join her in singing Happy Birthday to Scary.

Melanie C said: 'This is a very special award for us and it means a lot to be recognised for our writing and our music. It's great to recognised for writing zig-a-zig-ah!'

It really seemed that The Girls could do no wrong, but then, just before they began working on their film, disaster struck.

'SPICE GIRL FALLS OFF HER SHOE!' screamed the *Sun* headline. Followed by a story marked Exshoesive, it went on to tell how the day before, Emma, while on a trip to Istanbul to do a television show, had sprained an ankle when she toppled off her Buffalo platforms.

Baby was photographed coming home in a wheelchair and put the record straight the next day when she said: 'It was not the shoes. I was running out of the television studio and there was a big hole and my foot went down it. It was just a sprain and the bandages should be removed in a week.' The next day, when being carried out to a car by a minder, her sheep rucksack also had a matching bandage round its little foot.

As The Girls went into film production mode, the demands for interviews and access if anything increased, and I started to sound like a broken record, or like a lover with a persistent headache, consistent in the only answer I could give people, which was: No.

The feeling at Virgin was that we were in danger of over-exposure and we wanted to dampen things down for a few months. At least until we were ready with *Spiceworld*, their second album.

However, having spent a year building things up, we discovered this was one Genie who was not prepared to go back inside its bottle. Having successfully sold The Spice Girls to the tabloids, we found they weren't happy now unless they had their daily Spicey dish with which to feed their readers.

But after setting up some magazine covers that would coincide with the release of *Spiceworld*, it all began to catch up with me. I had been feeling ill for some time and was feeling increasingly burnt out. The mad schedule of the last year was beginning to take its toll. Handling The Spice Girls' press activities for a year had been the equivalent of five years compressed into a mad and completely exhausting twelve months.

My health was starting to suffer.

I went to see my GP, who took one look at me and declared: 'You should be in bed!' before issuing me with a sick note and advising me to get some rest.

A year living in Spiceworld had taken its toll. It was time to ignore my heart and listen to my body.

I handed in my notice.

On my last assignment with The Girls, well, with one of them, Melanie C, who was doing an interview for *Melody Maker*, I told her I was leaving and she gave me a sympathetic smile and said: 'You've had a really hard year, haven't you, Muff?'

It had been the most intense year of my life. The most exhilarating and, at the same time, the most exhausting year I have experienced. (So far!)

It was time to check-in with myself, take some time out to chill out and have a well-earned rest. It had been a roller-coaster of a year, one which had opened my eyes and one in which I had learnt a lot.

I will forever be grateful to The Girls for giving me the opportunity to share their world and the experience of a lifetime and I will always remember their enthusiasm, their earnest approach to life, their dedication and hard work.

You know you've made your mark with a job when your departure is reported on the international news. I was convalescing in a villa in Spain, when the headline came up on Sky News, who were reviewing the papers. They reported Matthew Wright's headline from that day's *Mirror*: 'SPICE GIRLS' PUBLICIST RETIRES DUE TO EXHAUSTION.'

By leaving, I had arrived.

EPILOGUE

In the glorious and frequently fickle world of pop, seven days can be a lifetime. And a year? That's an absolute eternity. Careers can be made or laid to rest in less time than it takes to make a video. And a year in Spiceworld? Well, that's something else again.

It is now twelve months since I left The Spice Girls, and during the time that I spent resting, writing this book, recharging my batteries and adjusting to life in the slow lane, the Famous Five continued to work as hard as ever, slogging their socks off, charging around the globe clocking up a million more air-miles, spending weeks in hair and make-up, breaking new records and gathering armfuls of awards in their wake. Zealously transporting themselves, their music and their inimitable manifesto to fans that number among them world leaders Nelson Mandela and Tony Blair, not forgetting the crowned heads of Europe, and dominating the news agenda while they did so.

Posh, Sporty, Ginger, Scary and Baby have experienced an unbelievably awesome time, with The Girls witnessing another whirlwind year that saw the release of their eagerly awaited second album *Spiceworld*, going straight to Number One all over the globe, notching up an awesome run of six Number One singles in the UK before they went on to break box-office records with their feature-film debut *Spiceworld – The Movie*. They then confounded the cynics and Noel Gallagher, by proving that they could sing beautifully and cut it live with a very slick and dazzling stage-show.

However, life was not to be without its problems. In November 1997, just minutes before the MTV awards ceremony, they sacked their manager, Simon Fuller. He had made them the most marketed band in history by tying them to innumerable sponsorship deals, with The Girls endorsing an avalanche of products from Pepsi to Polaroid and Walker's Crisps.

At the lectern, as The Girls, received the MTV European Award for Best Group and Geri dedicated it to Princess Diana – 'A true advocate of Girl Power!' – Melanie B informed the assembled glitterati that: 'Today is the happiest day of my life.'

Fuller's dismissal prompted a media backlash that was perhaps inevitable, given their saturation coverage over the preceding year, but which was marked by a decidedly viperish glee as journalists and media pundits did their best to pronounce the band finished. Even though at the time their album *Spiceworld* was a Number One album in almost every country in the world.

As we all know, the British have always maintained a strict adherence to the old 'Build 'em up, then knock 'em down' policy.

The Girls just got on with what they know how to do best: singing, dancing, and devotedly throwing themselves into their work.

Four weeks later, the relentless conjecture seemed to abate when HRH the Prince of Wales and the Princes William and Harry attended the premiere of *Spiceworld – The Movie* and Geri announced to reporters 'Charles is our new manager!'

He replied: 'Ah yes, but I'm very expensive.'

By now, The Girls were old hands when it came to the British royal family, having met Charles's mother, Queen Elizabeth, when performing for her at the sixty-ninth Royal Variety Performance two weeks earlier on 1 December.

This time no one got goosed. Nor was the Duke of Edinburgh subjected to the honorary Spice lipstick attack, which they deliver with relish each time they meet up with HRH Prince Charles.

Although looking embarrassed by their enthusiastic display of affection, you can tell the Prince loves every minute of it. No one is safe from a Spice lipstick attack. On that historic day in November when The Spice Girls accompanied Prince Charles on his trip to South Africa to visit Nelson Mandela, after Mr Mandela spookily echoed Melanie B's sentiments at the MTV Awards, by announcing that 'Today is the happiest day of my life!' he was seen having great wodges of Cherry Erotique lovingly removed by Scary, who dabbed his face with her hankie.

When The Spice Girls then became the first band in thirty-two years to capture the coveted Christmas Number One slot two years running, with the ballad 'Too Much', their critics in the UK were finally forced to admit that their gloomy predictions had been completely misjudged.

The *Guardian* even printed an apology in its Leader column, which stated: 'As our Prime Minister himself has proved, an institution which changes its mind merely proves its flexibility and modernity. We congratulate The Spice Girls on their success.'

At the end of May 1998, Geri Halliwell unexpectedly announced that she was leaving the group. Her sudden departure prompted more doom-mongering and fevered speculation from the media, but The Girls once again displayed their endearing sense of dedication and professionalism when they issued a joint statement with Geri's lawyer at a press conference in London. They informed the World's press that The Spice Girls would be carrying on without her as the Fab Four.

Within a day of her departure they were onstage in Oslo performing the last dates of their European tour with new arrangements and dance routines. A few days later, they performed with Pavarotti at a benefit concert for the War Child charity. It was very much business as usual.

Ginger's exit prompted a crisis among the plethora of tribute bands such as Nice 'n' Spicy and The Spicey Girls who all said they were going to have to sack one of their members!

At the end of that week Geri took stock at George Michael's villa in the South of France. And as I write, the rest of The Girls are in America where their new show is travelling coast to coast, playing to capacity crowds in stadiums and arenas for three months, where they will play a date at the prestigious Madison Square Gardens in New York, tickets for which had sold out in a record twelve minutes – a feat which in their time, not even the Rolling Stones or Led Zeppelin managed to pull off.

As I write, Geri's future plans are yet to be revealed, though by the time you have this book in your hands we will know which direction Geri's considerable talents have taken her.

And as for the other Spice Girls?

Well, it's obvious isn't it?

Girl Power is here to stay!